S0-BYK-460

Praise for *The Joyful Family*

"This book for parents, teachers, and professionals translates academic knowledge into pragmatic yet sophisticated suggestions to help children and families manage life's inevitable fears and adversity."

TIMOTHY F. DUGAN, M.D.,
Senior Consultant in Education, Cambridge Hospital,
Division of Child and Adolescent Psychiatry, Harvard Medical School,
and author of *The Child in Our Times*

"Dacey and Weygint deftly tackle a broad range of emotionally significant issues(from the mundane to the extraordinary, providing both specific activities and the invitation, encouragement, and framework from which readers can creatively build upon their examples. The authors' ideas for expanding the horizon of occasions for activities include ways of enhancing ordinary events, like the family meal, to anticipating major disasters, to practical suggestions for transforming the difficult duties of emotionally supporting ill friends and relatives into opportunities for forging and deepening emotional ties in one's community. This rich book made me reflect on my own parenting practices and gave me impetus to try their ideas very soon!"

ELIZABETH LIAO, M.D., child psychiatrist

"It was a pleasure to read two authors who so obviously love and respect families. From that love comes a wealth of ideas for improving the closeness, strength, and durability of families through the use of creative rituals. You will immediately want to try these ideas at home: create an altar; welcome a new baby; heal a rift; give blessings on a new venture. Creating your own celebrations will become an irresistible idea once you have read these clear instructions and great examples. My thanks to the authors for creating this rich resource."

ROBIN TARTAGLIA, Director, Lexington Community Education

"One of the best things parents can do is to foster effective and honest communication among all family members. This book is full of simple, creative ideas to help families celebrate events and make connections with each other in their own unique ways. Dacey and Weygint have drawn from rich resources that tie us to ancient structures and rhythms of human caring. They remind us of the value of repetition . . . as essential as the beating of our hearts. Parents can use this book to help create the joyfulness that naturally arises from safe, loving relationships."

LESLIE R. FENN, M.D., community psychiatrist

THE
Joyful
Family

THE Joyful Family

Meaningful Activities and Heartfelt Celebrations for
Connecting with the Ones You Love

John Dacey, Ph.D. and **Lynne Weygint**
Foreword by Will Glennon, author of *Fathering*

CONARI PRESS
Berkeley, California

Copyright © 2002 by John Dacey and Lynne Weygint

All Rights Reserved. No part of this book may be used or reproduced in any manner whatsoever without written permission, except in the case of brief quotations in critical articles or reviews. For information, contact: Conari Press, 2550 Ninth Street, Suite 101, Berkeley, CA 94710-2551.

Page 213: "Song (4)" from *Collected Poems: 1957–1982* by Wendell Berry. Copyright © 1985 by Wendell Berry. Reprinted by permission of North Point Press, a division of Farrar, Straus and Giroux, LCC.

Conari Press books are distributed by Publishers Group West.

ISBN: 1-57324-572-0

Cover Photography: Ross Anania, Bronwyn Kidd, Jim Arbogast,
    Keith Brofsky/Photodisc
Cover Design: Claudia Smelser
Book Design and Composition: Crowfoot Design

Library of Congress Cataloging-in-Publication Data
Dacey, John S.
    The joyful family : meaningful activities and heartfelt celebrations for connecting with the ones you love / John Dacey, Lynne Weygint; foreword by Will Glennon.
        p.   cm.
    Includes bibliographical references and index.
    ISBN 1-57324-572-0
    1. Family. 2. Ritual. 3. Manners and customs. 4. Parent and child.
    I. Weygint, Lynne. II. Title.
HQ734 .D2 2002
646.7'8—dc21
                                    2001005475
Printed in Canada.
01 02 03 TC 10 9 8 7 6 5 4 3 2 1

This book is dedicated with much love to:

*The first people to introduce me
to the power of ceremony and celebration,
my DeLorme aunts: Irma McDonough,
Rita Stein, Emily Haley, Ann Castelli,
Pat DeLorme, and my great aunt Agnes McElhill.*

JOHN DACEY

*My joyful family:
My mother for bringing a lifetime of
delightful rituals into my childhood,
my father for giving me my very first journal at age ten,
my sister for always being there for me, and, of course,
my wonderful husband, Pat, and our sons, Willie and Jamie,
who always put up with my crazy ideas.*

LYNNE WEYGINT

The Joyful Family

Foreword
by Will Glennon, author of *Fathering*

The "Family," as in the institution, has taken a real beating over the last few decades. From one side we have ominous statistics cited about everything from the divorce rate and the rise of single-parent households to absent fathers and the perils of latchkey kids. From the other side we have disquieting stories about the seemingly ever-growing number of dysfunctional families. To listen to all the commentary, one could easily get the impression that after thousands of years of success as the vehicle for renewing the population, raising children into adults, and providing some semblance of support, love, and nurturing along the way, the "Family" has suddenly stopped working altogether.

Needless to say, things aren't quite that bad. The family, be it the smaller version of mother, father, and children or the larger extended version of grandparents, aunts, uncles, and cousins, has been the primary social unit since the dawn of our evolution, and it continues to be just that—only in ever-increasing variations. In consideration of its exquisite ability to evolve and adapt, the family is not only alive and well but, in many ways, thriving. In that light, it is not the deficiencies of the family that are striking but its incredible enduring strength.

That is not to dismiss the truly monumental changes underway. The family is still strong—it's just that in the last seventy-five years or so the context within which the family exists has changed dramatically. Moving in such a short period of time from a predominantly rural lifestyle, where families resided within the comforting habitual cycle of seasonal duties and obligations, into our current vastly accelerated world has completely changed the nature, the number, and the magnitude of influences impacting family life. These days, our schedules are so stretched by demands from outside the family that it can seem that what we experience as a family happens on a haphazard basis. We are losing our small but deeply connecting rituals as well as our larger and more elaborate family traditions. We are losing them not because we don't value them but because we are not paying enough attention as they are slowly being undermined by television, telephones, rush hour, demanding careers, e-mail, fast food, and the astounding mobility of the twenty-first century. We are all, from parents to children to extended family members and cherished friends, moving too fast and in too many directions at once, and unless we sit down and consciously create new traditions, we are in danger of losing one of the most precious gifts of being a family.

Against that backdrop, John Dacey and Lynne Weygint have done us a great service by helping us to revive family traditions and rituals. These powerful and precious recurring moments within our family make up one of the core elements that give our families strength and depth. Throughout most of our history, many of the simplest daily chores of life—lighting the morning fire, feeding the domestic animals, gathering together at the evening meal, mending clothes and tools, sharing stories—took on ritual importance simply through reassuring repetition. With *The Joyful Family*, the authors have given us a very practical and wonderfully supportive guide for creating our own strategy to bring more meaning into our interactions. *The Joyful Family* helps us rebuild family traditions and rituals to revitalize our sense of connection in a way tailored for our own lives.

As I write these words, I am smiling as I think back to "English muffin pizza night." It was one of many small traditions my family created, lasting only a few years in time but reverberating still now with incredible warmth and power. On "pizza" night, my entire family would gather in front of our '50s-era fold-up dinner trays and eat "English muffin pizza" (the menu never varied) while watching *Bonanza* and *Have Gun Will Travel* on our spanking new 13-inch black-and-white television set. There was also the annual Fourth of July gathering of the extended clan, which required an early dawn beach landing to stake out the best spot. Dozens of other traditions large and small were part of my growing-up days. Now, forty years later, these moments make up the structure of my family memories, dominate the stories told and retold at family gatherings, and provide the glue that binds us so tightly together.

The Joyful Family should be handed out to new parents as they leave the delivery room so that they can all, consciously and with deliberation, begin to build powerful threads of love and connection in their families. This is a book that can be turned to again and again to honor everything from the birth of a child to his or her high school graduation to all the everyday and wondrous moments in between.

chapter 1

Making a Family Joyful

D o you belong to a joyful family? Does your family have a happy sense of connection most of the time? Or do you sometimes wish that you had a greater feeling of togetherness, of cohesion?

It isn't easy to have a joyful family today. Many people, especially mothers, are struggling to keep their families from fragmenting. Despite these efforts, family members live more and more in their own separate worlds, unwilling or unable to help each other deal with a stressful society. There are many forces that seem bent on disintegrating family unity. Although the American family is not as endangered as some would have us believe, worry about it is widespread.

The future need not be so grim, though. *All* families, whether traditional—"one mom, one dad, two sibs"—or nontraditional—"two grandparents, one granddaughter"—can relieve stress. A well-conceived ritual can provide a wonderful antidote to external stressors. As a part of our professional work (teaching psychology and organizational skills, family counseling), we have observed many families over the years. Those that are joyful always seem to have two factors in common: (1) They deal effectively with the critical moments in the family's life; and (2) they enhance each member's sense of belonging. Such families know how to work through the hard times that we all face and, just as important, celebrate the good ones. They are truly joyful.

Generally speaking, though, the quality of family rituals in Western countries has been declining in recent decades. For example, people used to discuss issues that were important in their lives over their evening meal or while sitting on their front porches after dinner. Most of us don't do that anymore. We might like to, but other demands seem to get in the way. Obviously, not all of those conversations made for better lives, but at least the opportunity was there. Today, the average family eats together twice a week. Over 40 percent of homes have the television set on during dinner. The average father spends about ten minutes each day in conversation with each of his children. The average mother, especially if she works outside the home, doesn't do much better.

Our national summer holidays also seem to have lost their power to bring us together. In earlier times, families used Memorial Day, the Fourth of July, and Labor Day as special occasions to seriously consider the reasons those days were set aside. Parades, games, and picnics were ornate affairs participated in by all.

Now, for most of us, a holiday is little more than a welcome day off from work, with everyone spending the time to meet her or his individual needs. Don't get us wrong. We are not urging that everyone return to "the good old days." You couldn't do that even if you wanted to, and there were lots of ways that the good old days were not so great, too. Instead, we believe that families can gain marvelous benefits from inventing their own new rituals or by carefully redesigning older ones.

Most families would like to be joyful. Intuitively, if not consciously, almost everyone dreams of being part of a cohesive, supportive, loving group, one that fosters abilities and values. The goal of this book is to help bring that dream to fruition. We suggest that this goal can be reached through the use of well-designed family ceremonies. As Dr. Robin Chernoff of the Johns Hopkins Children's Center has said, "Rituals strengthen family bonds, and they also forge a link between the family you came from and the one you're creating." They do so, she has found, by creating character, providing security, and fostering maturity.

What Is a Ritual?

By *ritual*, we mean a ceremony that is intended to celebrate the good times and promote the healing process after the bad. It is a rite that prescribes in detail what each person should do and when. Each time a ritual is repeated, a tradition is built up and honored once again. Thus traditions are ceremonies that have become habitual.

The funeral service, a commemoration found in societies around the world and throughout human history, models the value of ritual. The funeral is designed to give us the strength to deal with our grief and to transition back to a focus on life and its daily routine. Anthropologist William Bridges distinguishes between "change" and "transition." Change comes when a surviving person realizes that she will no longer be able to see a loved one who has died. The ability to accept the death, however, to come to terms with it and move on with one's life, is what Bridges means by *transition*. Ritual can often facilitate a successful transition.

Rituals may be characterized by the rules that you establish for them. Syracuse University researcher Barbara Friese suggests that you and your family answer the following questions about each of your ritual designs:

- *Will this rite require a lot of planning* every time you carry it out, or will you just "go with the flow"?

- *Are the elements of your ritual systematically well defined?* That is, will everyone know exactly what to do? Should everyone know what implements (a candle, reading) to use and where to sit (stand, kneel)?

- *Will it be regular?* Will you always hold it in the same place? At the same time? For the same duration?

- *Will it be important that everyone take the ceremony seriously,* or will a more relaxed attitude prevail?

- *Are family members expected to be emotionally as well as intellectually involved?* For example, will people be encouraged to express their feelings?

- *How frequently will the ritual occur?* Weekly, monthly, every other Tuesday night?

- *Will it be important that everyone come to every session?* Will there be a penalty for not coming? Might those who attend feel irritated at those who don't make it?

- *Will the rite be highly regimented?* Will it be performed the same way every time?

- *Will the ritual be permanent?* Do you believe that your children are likely to continue it when they become adults?

There are no correct answers to these questions; it depends on what works best for your family in any particular situation. There *are* ramifications to each of the various answers you give, however. For example, if it really doesn't matter whether family members attend the ceremony, the power of its effect will almost certainly be weakened, and there is a good chance that it will be dropped eventually. That might be all right with your family, but it is one of the important questions you can raise when you are creating your design.

Following is a more specific example from Lynne's life of what we mean by family-designed rituals.

One of Lynne's Invented Rituals

My family and I first began our ceremonial life together when I decided that a weekly family meeting might help us communicate and plan our frenetic schedules better. We entered the world of ritual completely unaware that that was what we were doing. Somewhere in the vagueness of my thinking, I guess I hoped we might feel closer as a family if we had regular meetings. I especially hoped that we might draw in our eleven-year-old son; our six-year-old son was already an actively involved member of our little group. Once such a central force in our bond, our older son was becoming a satellite in an orbit that moved elliptically away from the rest of us. I knew he was growing up and that early adolescence is a time of questioning. It was the distancing that disturbed me. At the time, it really didn't occur to me that we might create a meaningful rite.

The spiritual aspects of connecting regularly and purposefully with my family eluded me. I was marching forward, as I tend to do, blind to the richness of the opportunities ritual offers. As you might imagine, our first family meetings, designed and led by me, were barely satisfactory. Yes, we planned our week as a group. We met, we talked, we looked at the crowded calendar. The boys teased and were bored, my husband and I tensed and almost gave up. Another good idea that hadn't worked. Or so we thought.

Two years and approximately 100 family meetings later, I'm so glad—we're all so glad—that we didn't give up on our "meetings" and thus on each other! Our meetings evolved from their original purpose into what we celebrate today: a weekly time for shared renewal, our Sabbath, our unique ceremony.

We each contribute. Our leader lights a tall, thick candle, bringing a warm glow to this small and cozy spot—our only real gathering room. We sit in silence (occasionally broken by boyish giggles) and enjoy the warmth for a too-brief moment. The leader may open with a thought (this seems more popular with the grown-ups in our tiny group) or may move directly into thank-you's, compliments, and appreciations.

I'm often surprised by the richness in this sharing. The little things that seemingly go unnoticed each day now become the kindnesses that reinforce our family bond. Often, one person's appreciation of another reminds us all of other gestures we had forgotten. So we go around the circle again, and sometimes a third time.

Next, we discuss any problems that have arisen during the week or that have not been solved from previous meetings. These problems can be anything from a scheduling conflict to a friendship in distress to a request for "better" (less nutritious) after-school snacks.

Our older son was quick to see the advantages of this style of problem solving and soon began training his parents. Now, when one of us launches into a tirade about showing respect for a teacher he dislikes, he is apt to interrupt with, "I think we should discuss this at family meeting instead of taking the time now." Of course, his intent is to avoid the lecture entirely, but discussion about respect will be on the agenda for the next meeting. When the topic comes up on the following Sunday night, the ensuing conversation tends to be less heated, more thoughtful, and more general. By then, it is about respect for all, not just a certain student's relationship with a particular teacher.

Finally, we review the calendar, briefly discuss family finances (something I hope to develop more as the children get older), look at the week's chores, and discuss the family's fun activity for the following week. The leader closes the meeting with a song, a short reading, or both. We always enjoy a final moment of silence in the candlelight before dessert.

As if by magic, this ritual, evolving out of a singular need for a more ordered schedule, has made our family more joyful. We arrive at our meeting as four individuals with different lives; we leave as a family, bonded by understanding and forgiveness, humanity and love.

One of the best uses of family rites is bridging the gap between generations. Here's how John went about trying to achieve this goal.

One of John's Invented Rituals

For the past seven years, my wife and I have taken care of our five grandchildren on Fridays from 9 A.M. to 1 P.M. so that their mothers can carry out their part-time jobs. Finding activities that are constructive and yet fun to do can challenge the imagination. Two years ago, as a part of our routine, I decided to design a new ceremony that would entertain and educate the older children while their young cousins took their morning nap.

On the back of our property, we have an 8' x 10' shed that served as a workshop and tool storage area. I removed the back wall and replaced it with two large windows overlooking the woods, so that I could have a place conducive to thinking and writing. In the center of the cabin I installed a miniature pot-bellied wood stove to provide heat in winter. For several years now we have used this shed as the setting for our rituals. Although at first most of the ideas were mine, gradually the kids had more and more say in what we would do. Soon going out to "our cabin" became a regular part of our Friday schedule.

I have several chairs facing the windows. From the top of the window frames, I have hung two crystals, and when the sun is shining, the walls and ceiling of the cabin are covered with dozens of little gyrating rainbows. The children love them. Even when it is raining, they are content for a while to watch what is happening out in the woods. Across one of the windows, I have built a shelf with a molding attached to the edges that holds the half-inch of sand I spread across the shelf. My five-year-old grandson loves to rake the sand with a toy garden rake to make it look like a Japanese meditation garden. We take turns placing our favorite small objects on the sand and then telling each other stories about them. I have put a little bowl at one end, and at the beginning of our sessions, I light a small piece of sage and let it smolder a bit. It creates a lovely calming aroma in the cabin. On winter days, we sometimes roast hot dogs for lunch.

A variation on our cabin tradition we call "wondering time." Each of us takes turns saying, "I wonder why . . . ?" Anyone who wants to venture an answer is encouraged to do so. This activity almost always generates interesting conversations. In fact, this whole Friday morning tradition fosters good talks and good feelings. Perhaps most important, I think it is creating some wonderful memories for us all.

Spiritual Growth

Although this book is not about spiritual growth per se, spirituality plays a central role in a number of the celebrations and commemorations we describe (have you ever noticed that the word *spiritual* contains the word *ritual?*) Roy Oswald, in his excellent book *Transforming Rituals,* describes the ultimate life transition: spiritual growth. Such a transformation, he says, is usually a painful process, as is most change. "It is not that we resist change but that we resist loss." Most of us, Oswald claims, have a number of "losses that we may not even be aware we are grieving, as well as a number of new beginnings that we may never have acknowledged and celebrated. We experience the resulting stresses and strains. How can we capture the possibilities change offers for individual and communal transformation, and reduce the physical, emotional, and spiritual casualties of change?" His answer is that we need to redesign old rituals and invent new ones. Rituals "allow us to go beyond words. They help us express who we are as individuals and the way we want our lives to unfold. They express our belonging to a specific family, tribe, ethnic group, nationality, religious tradition, or denomination. Finally, they remind us that we live as part of the entire community of humanity who share this earth."

Recent polls have been finding a heightened interest in spirituality. People are raising questions about the meanings and purposes of life and death. This is related to changes in attitudes toward organized religion. In the 1960s and '70s, baby boomers in great numbers left the religions in which they were raised. One study found that among that age group, 61 percent of fundamentalist Protestants, 67 percent of Catholics, 69 percent of moderate Protestants, and 84 percent of Jews stopped practicing their religions. In the 1990s, many of them tried reengaging in the religion of their youth, but a majority still found it unsatisfactory. On the other hand, spirituality, especially as practiced in non-organizational settings, is making huge inroads on the public consciousness. For example, the topic of spirituality is the fastest growing sector of the publishing industry. Although our book is not primarily concerned with spirituality, many of the rituals we recommend have a spiritual component, or easily could have.

Most families engage in rituals, at least occasionally. Vacations, Sunday afternoon dinner, family reunions, weddings, holidays, first days of school, birthdays, graduations, family prayers—all are examples of household rituals. The kinds of situations in which rites may be used effectively are limited only by the imagination of family members. Here's an example:

Making a Full Recovery

At age fifty-nine, Li Pac felt like a very old man. His right hip had "rusted out," as he put it, and for several years he had been forced to hobble about, feeling elderly before his time. Six months ago it had taken him fifreen minutes to get up the stairs to his bedroom. Eventually he was unable to climb the stairs at all.

He resisted having hip surgery until he realized that he could no longer play with his three grandchildren: Gregory, seven; Ellen, four; and little Damian, two. For nearly half a year, he had been unable to even pick them up in his arms, which he dearly loves to do. One day several months before the surgery, as he was walking down the street with Damian, a dog came bounding toward them. His little grandson, panicked by the sight, turned to him with arms upraised, crying, "Grandpa Li, Grandpa Li, quick, pick me up!"

"Honey, I'm sorry but I just can't!"

"But . . . but . . . Grandpa, you got to!"

Stepping in front of the child, Li had shouted menacingly at the dog, driving it away. The child was safe, but Li had felt like an incompetent old has-been. What if his bad hip had prevented him from protecting his grandson?

This and several other deflating incidents seemed well behind him now. The hip-replacement surgery had taken care of that. It took a lot of courage and pain to get up and walk again, but somehow he had. Now he has been home from the rehabilitation hospital for a week, and his grandchildren have visited him daily. Their high-pitched encouragement has been music to his ears, spurring him on to keep working at his exercises.

Now the day that he has been looking forward to so much has finally come: the doctor has said it will be okay if he picks up Damian. Depending on his body's reaction to lifting the boy, Li will be allowed to try to pick up Ellen, too. His daughter knows what a huge step forward this will be for him. "We really should do something special to honor this momentous occasion," she thinks to herself. "It's such a big deal to him, and we need to recognize that. But how do you design a 'picking-up-a-kid' ceremony?"

How indeed? Should it be like a birthday party, with candles and presents? Should special foods be served? Should someone give a little speech? How should the ceremony be recorded so that it becomes part of the family's history? Does it matter if the ritual is held facing a certain direction of the compass? In the chapters that follow, we will provide you with examples of many kinds of rituals, so that you will have a much better idea of how to proceed with yours.

The Design of This Book

The Joyful Family is organized into fifteen chapters. In the first three, we explain the nature of family ceremonies and the ingredients needed to make them work. We explore the concept of ritual, the ancient elements that still can make a rite work well, and the special role that altars and amulets can play.

The next eleven chapters describe models of rituals designed for two purposes:

1. Enhancing each family member's sense of belonging; for instance, recognizing your family's cultural and religious heritage, bridging the gap between the generations, and making every day special.

2. Handling the difficult times in our lives; for instance, resolving misunderstandings, supporting an ill member of the family, and honoring departed family members.

In the final chapter, we present some techniques that can help your family be more imaginative as you design your own ceremonies. At the end of the book, we provide a resource guide to help you explore further.

We really have only one goal in mind: We hope our book will help you make your family more cohesive and joyful.

chapter 2

The Essential Components of Family Ritual

Humans have been using rituals for such a long time that we seldom question *why* we use them as we do. We gather for Shabbat dinner, for a birthday party, for Christmas morning. We light candles, we sing songs, we prepare special foods. Typically, we take the process for granted.

The majority of our ceremonies—the new ones we've recently developed and the ones that have survived for centuries—are made up of a few basic components. Not many of us understand or know the history or meaning behind these components. It isn't essential that you do—you and your family can design an imaginative and effective rite without knowing anything about the history of the process. We think, though, that you may find that your invented rituals are richer if you know more about the nature of these principles: the four ancient quadrants, the concepts of the circle and the spiral, the role of repetition, and the basics of family communications.

The Role of the Four Ancient Quadrants

Native Americans have long used their knowledge of the earth and the natural world to invent ceremonies that served them well for centuries. For example, most North American tribes had rites based on their knowledge of the land and its elements to help them resolve interpersonal conflicts. We think it makes sense for us to try to gain from this experience, as well as from the combined wisdom of all the peoples in the world who have gone before us. Fascinatingly, there is remarkable agreement in the lore of ancient peoples about what comprises a well-designed ritual. The best path for creating such a ceremony, we believe, lies in honoring these traditions, while at the same time putting most of your energy into progressive new ideas. Here are two examples of what we mean.

There is a way that these concepts can be useful to you and your family. When you go to a play, you often find that the program makes statements like "Act Two—the next morning," or "Two weeks have passed." You know that when the curtain opens on the second act, only moments have passed in real time. In order to understand the play, however, you need to suspend judgment and let yourself believe that the time specified has really gone by. If you don't, you will not be able to grasp and fully enjoy the effect the playwright is trying to achieve. We suggest, then, that you suspend judgment about the traditional components of rituals so that you can readily draw from their power and effectiveness.

Ancient peoples, as well as many cultures today, have seen life as a circle made up of four wedges, or quadrants. Each of the quadrants consists of a set of associated components. In each of the sets, there is a direction of the compass, one of the four basic elements as described by the early Greeks, a season of the agricultural year, and a stage of life. The quadrants are as follows:

- East, air, spring/planting (which begins at the spring equinox, in the third week of March), and birth/childhood

- South, fire, summer/growth (the summer solstice, the third week of June), and youth/young adulthood

- West, water, autumn/harvest (the fall equinox, the third week of September), and maturity/middle age

- North, earth, winter/die-off (the winter solstice, the third week of December), elderhood/death-rebirth

"The Components of Ritual" depicts the relationships among the four quadrants.

The Components of Ritual

North
Earth
Winter/Die-off
Elderhood and
Death-Rebirth

West
Water
Autumn/Harvest
Maturity and
the Middle Years

East
Air
Spring/Planting
Birth and
Childhood

South
Fire
Summer/Growth
Youth and
Young Adulthood

The Traditional Components

Most ancient traditions accept the idea that the four directions of the compass are also the gateways to four spiritual worlds. The North, for instance, represents the mysterious land of our inner selves. North is the place of serious, sober concerns. We might orient ourselves to the North when dealing with the loss of a loved one, when getting in touch with feelings of grief, and when beginning the process of healing (rebirth). The East is the land of new beginnings, the South symbolizes vibrant youth, and the West is the place of serenity and wisdom.

The ancient Greeks believed that everything in the world was made up of combinations of four natural elements: earth, air, fire, and water. We now understand that there are 103 basic elements, and more may be discovered. Nevertheless, if we accept the Greek view as metaphor rather than fact, and recognize that the four elements are still vital components of many existing ceremonies, we can gain from the experience of our forebears. The four elements are much in evidence in a Catholic funeral, for instance. There is water (the sprinkling of holy water on the casket); fire (the lit candles); air (a smell of the incense burning in the censor); and earth (which is tossed on the casket at the burial site). This rite has lasted unchanged for a very long time and has served a great many people during one of the greatest hardships in life, the death of a loved one.

Why should the four elements be linked to the four directions? Couldn't air go just as well with South, for example? Well, fire seems to go with South because the southern quadrant is the warmest area in the Northern Hemisphere, and is symbolic of the idea that there is more "fire" in the veins of youth and young adults than in any other age group. But in reality, no one really knows why or how these pairings have come about. The reasons are lost in ancient history. Perhaps we ought just take them on faith.

In designing your rituals, it is not necessary that you organize the elements together according to our components table. In fact, we think you'll find that by combining them in different ways, using the imaginations of all the participants in your rites, you may find a spark of creative inspiration. Too, you might like to be guided by the traditional until you gain more experience in ritual design. And these concepts are useful in a variety of ways. For instance, they give us guidance in:

- Setting up the physical space of a ceremony
- Deciding how to decorate the space
- What to think about when we're designing an altar
- Writing introductory statements
- Picking out the sounds, scents, and lighting that accent our rites.

In what follows, we offer a brief description of the symbolic meaning of the quadrants (the spiral design in the center of the table will be explained later in this chapter).

East, Air, Spring/Planting, Birth and Childhood

The sun rising in the East as a symbol of new beginnings corresponds naturally to spring planting, birth, and early childhood. The famous anthropologist Joseph Campbell pointed out that many cultures have a myth of the journey of life, which almost always begins its travel from an easterly direction. The great circle journey, taken by a hero or heroine traveling around the compass seeking wisdom, is an example. It is probably no accident that the word *East* is included in our springtime holiday, Easter. In traditional lore, the year begins not on January 1, but on March 21, the time of the spring equinox and the approximate date of Easter, with its theme of rebirth. Therefore rituals designed to celebrate the key changes in life, such as a baby's birth and first step, or a decadal birthday, could be oriented toward the East.

Closely related to the concept of new beginnings is the notion of growth and revitalization. It is in the spring when winter's icy grip on the land and its frozen waters is loosened; seedlings begin to sprout and the Earth seems to come alive again. March winds blow a fresh new atmosphere of change across our lives. One of the most important beginnings is our birth, marked by our first intake of air. Therefore, air is aligned with East. In Native American traditions, the East is the home of "The Great Breath," a term they sometimes used for God. According to the Old Testament, the beginning of human life occurred when God breathed air into Adam's body. Inhalation is symbolic of another associated concept, inspiration.

Symbolism and Examples of Air

Element	Symbolism	Examples
Air	Buoyancy	Wind
	Lightness	Balloons
	Freedom	Kites
	Inspiration	Chimes
	Speech and laughter	
	Bubbles	
	Music	

South, Fire, Growth, Youth and Young Adulthood

In traditional lore, the South is associated with creativity and strength because youth and young adulthood are the times in our lives when we are at peak strength. In the Northern Hemisphere, the South is the land of heat, of fertilization, of sexuality. The sun is at full strength. Thus, South is also paired with the element of fire and with the agricultural cycle of rapid growth.

The budding of spring gives way to the full bloom of summer. It is a time of wakefulness and hard work. The long days of summer allow for more work to be done. By long-established custom, South is the direction our ancestors faced when they wanted to react to an important change in family circumstances, such as the marriage of a young adult daughter, and when they wanted to deal with environmental catastrophes such as pestilence and great fires. Rites dealing with crises, solving specific problems, and improving school-related issues could be oriented toward the South.

The fertility of the soul and body are also symbolized here. A yogic expert, Margie McCarthy, explains, "On the level of our physical bodies, our sexual fires are representative. Within our bodies, it is the coiled, sleeping serpent-dragon, the goddess power known in yoga as Kundalini, which awakens and rises up, uncoiling through the chakras, bringing awakening and enlightenment as she passes." In yoga, the chakras are the seven centers along the spinal column from the base of the spine to the top of the head. In the yogic tradition, the smooth flow of energy (heat) and information through these centers is what brings about effective living.

Symbolism and Examples of Fire

Element	Symbolism	Examples
Fire	Warmth/destruction	Bonfires
	Passion	Candles
	Magic	Campfires
	Love	Sunlight
	Creativity	Spicy food
	Fireplaces, woodstoves	
	Flashlights	

West, Water, Autumn/Harvest, Maturity and the Middle Years

The West is the place of brave deeds. It is where the adult's growing maturity allows for increased courage and daring. Reaping the fruits of all the learning that comes from the efforts made earlier in life, middle-aged people are able to consolidate what they have gained and take chances with life that previously would have been too risky. In the West, dreams may be fulfilled and a sense of productivity prevails. Ceremonies oriented in a westerly direction are useful, for example, for celebrating achievements, bridging the gap between generations, and for clarifying personal and family values.

Water is the element that predominates in this quadrant. Water has a number of characteristics that can be useful to the ritual designer. It is nourishing, cooling, cleansing, and is often used in blessings. It is the symbol for emotionality, but especially for the smooth flow of emotions. By the release of emotions—through crying, for example—we are able to calm ourselves. When we are immersed in water, our hearts beat more slowly, a reflection of the fact that we are descended from fish. The growing popularity of tabletop waterfalls is probably the result of our desire to become more tranquil at work and at home. The ability to calm the nervous system is essential when we wish to be brave and to take chances with life.

Although this is the time of autumn and the harvest (also associated with the West), it is also a time for preparing for death. This is the quadrant for endings, and it is usually used in rites for marking milestones, dealing with terminal illness, and for making every day special.

Symbolism and Examples of Water

Element	Symbolism	Examples
Water	Baptism	Waterfall
	Cleansing	Soap suds
	Change	Oils
	Birth	Rain
	Playfulness	Waves

North, Earth, Winter/Die-off, Elderhood and Death

The North is the land of mystery and the unseen, the home of the afterlife. Our ancestors viewed the North (especially the far North) as a place of stillness and frozen tranquility. The Earth in winter also seems a time of daydreaming and contemplation, of the search for wisdom. Winter is a time when things are quiet, sometimes quite literally, since the snow serves to muffle sounds. North is also connected with the power of silence, a place of listening, of knowing when and when not to speak, and of keeping secrets. These qualities can be most helpful in family rituals, especially those in which we try to solve specific family problems and bridge the gap between generations. Those are situations in which listening, holding back hurtful words, and speaking words of thanks and encouragement are extremely important. Such actions help to form bonds of trust among family members.

Funerals and grief are often related to this darkest hour. Earth, of course, plays an important role in the way that we think about death. Many people believe it is natural to return to the earth from which we have come. At burials, we throw earth on the casket as a symbol of our acceptance of our loss.

Although in the early afternoon the sunlight starts to fade, at midnight the light begins its return to the land, which will be completed with the coming of dawn. This is why initiations are often held in the middle of the night, whether by athletes as an induction onto the team, by college fraternities for membership in the club, or by pre-industrial societies for inclusion into the comradeship of adult men. In pre-industrial ceremonies, there is often an attempt to teach the young men that what lies beyond death is birth, that after the end of a cycle there is a beginning. In many North/earth/winter ceremonies, there is the opportunity to see birth *in* the death, to see the beginning while you are at the end. This is the central point in rituals designed to honor departed family members—they are dead, but still they can have a beneficial influence.

Associating the North and winter with old age is common, but not necessarily correct. As Grey Wolf notes in his book, *Earth Signs,* Native American tradition typically recognizes the elders of the tribe for their wisdom, but the elders are not necessarily old in years. Grey Wolf explains that younger men and women may also possess enlightenment, which is always the beginning of a new understanding. Wisdom is associated with winter because it is a time of rest and reflection.

Symbolism and Examples of Earth

Element	Symbolism	Examples
Earth	Solidity	Soil
	Heartiness	Ashes
	Burial	Wood
	Afterlife	Rocks, stones
	Darkness	Minerals
		Growth/Plants
		Clay
		Crystals

Circles and Spirals ◎

One way to look at life is that it is like a river, flowing in a relatively straight line from point *A* to point *B*. Most typical life events are reasonable, with each event following its predecessor in a more or less predictable sequence. For example, if you were to read a biography of Abraham Lincoln, you would most likely find the account of his life to be logical, rational, and sequential. This is known as the linear way of thinking. You think this way partly because your life is pervaded by the media, which tends to organize stories into neat, orderly passages. The linear thought process also is reinforced by the amazing advances obtained as a result of science. Scientists tend to see reality as a series of circumstances, with event *A* causing event *B,* and the events *B, C,* and *D* combining to cause event *E,* and so on.

It has not always been this way. Rather than seeing life as happening along a straight line, beginning with birth and ending with death, humans used to view their existence as being *circular.* For example, "We are created out of dust and when we die, to dust we return—we come full circle." An obvious example of circularity is the rotation of the seasons that even today so dominates the lives of farmers, hunters, and fishermen. For millennia, subsistence was seen as a never-ending circle revolving through the vagaries of winter, spring, summer, and fall. Life is followed by death, which is followed by new life. Sunrise, sunset—'round and 'round go the hands of the clock, recording the continuity of our essence.

From the sun-wheels found in Neolithic rock engravings to the huge lotus flowers said to have held both Buddha and Brahma, the circle has been a powerful symbol. It is reflected in the haloes of Christ and the Christian saints. The Celtic religions used the circle as a symbol of their main god, the sun. In his efforts to convert the Irish Celts, Saint Patrick combined the circle with the cross to form the Celtic cross.

The use of the principle of circularity in ceremonies is limited because it is only two-dimensional. But when we add a vertical dimension to a circle, we have a spiral. A spiral is a curved line that extends vertically through space. It is much more analogous to most life events than is either a straight line or a circle. For example, when we go through the seasons of the year from spring to spring, we do not circle back to the same conditions from which we started. The second spring is more like the first than it is like winter, but it is never the same spring.

A married couple, like two planets in orbit, move away from each other and then back toward each other again. It is hoped that as they circle about each other, they grow upward, deepening their mutual understanding and love. It is said that the course of true love never runs straight. Instead it spirals higher in quality, with many variations along the way. If, on the other hand, as the couple gets to know each other better they discover that they don't like what they find, then their relationship disintegrates in a downward spiral.

Spirals permeate our lives, from the double helix of our DNA to the social patterns of our relationships. In ancient yogic tradition, energy flows in the spiral from the lowest chakra at the base of our spine (emotions, sexuality) up to the highest at the top of our heads (thoughts, wisdom). So it could be with rituals. As we design and re-design, we keep the elements that work well and experiment with ways to improve them. This process invites greater complexity and richness.

The spiral is a symbol of an important attitude toward rites: You cannot expect to have overnight success. Your path toward your goals will often wind across and intermingle with other paths your family is already following. In fact, one of the chief functions of rituals has always been to help us close the gaps between ourselves and others, to help us achieve more dynamic connections with each other. Such interaction occurs when we let go of the intellectual, linear way of thinking, and allow ourselves to be taken over, at least to some extent, by our feelings. Feelings by their nature tend to be nonlinear. They oscillate in waves and spiral back around on themselves, sometimes without obvious rhyme or reason. Descriptions of the ceremonies of ancient and "primitive" cultures are filled with images of participants moving in circular and snake-like patterns. It seems as though they understood the power these shapes have in evoking emotional responses. Getting in better touch with honest emotions—our own and each other's—can frequently lead to new and better ways of thinking. Attaining these rewards usually takes some time, however.

In summary, we do not merely repeat ceremonial activities—each time we add something, we move from a simple to a more complex expression of the objective. If you have patience, you will make slow but steady progress, winding your way toward your ultimate goal of becoming a more cohesive and happy family.

Repetition

The repeated use of simple, clear ideas can work powerfully on participants. Symbols (such as the aroma of the candles, the color of the altar cloth, the items placed on the altar) may provoke an array of meanings more efficiently than do words. Repetition, therefore, can produce powerful benefits. It is important that you and your family understand the ways in which the reiterative use of symbols works. As a simple example, you might want to start each of your family meetings with a brief statement or prayer, such as, "May our family grow closer in wisdom and love." As family members *repeat* this line on a weekly basis, it may begin subconsciously to affect their relationships with each other.

Rituals often prove most effective because the repetitive use of their symbols has imprinted a central message (for example, we need to think more about the nature of our values) into the psyches of family members. *Thus the ritual becomes a tradition,* and it is in our traditions that we find the best chance for creating lasting connections. In chapters 4 through 14, we offer activities that incorporate this concept of repetition.

Family Communication

In all of the ceremonies described in this book, the ability to communicate effectively is of paramount importance. It is crucial that *all* members play an active role in developing and carrying out the rituals. Each individual must feel comfortable discussing feelings and concerns and feel confident that her input is welcome.

Going Beyond Rigid Roles

Several research studies have indicated that the interactions taking place in most family rituals do not meet the criteria described in the previous paragraph. Let's take the typical evening meal as an example. The average American family eats dinner together only two times a week. Not only is the *number* of family dinners diminishing, but the *quality* of the interactions at these meals is often so poor that it is questionable as to whether they should even be called ceremonies. The typical American dinner at home frequently involves no more conversation than an occasional "Please pass the potatoes," "How was your day?" or "What did you do at school today?" "Nothing."

In families where one or both of the parents are alcoholics or drug abusers, investigators have found an almost total absence of rites. It appears that the children and the spouse are usually so fearful about disturbing the drinker/abuser that gatherings of any kind are avoided.

Everyone quietly goes her or his own way, hoping to keep the peace. This absence of regular interactions causes personality problems. For instance, the children of alcoholics have been found to be more anxious, compulsive, and consumed with self-disgust than their peers.

Family theorists Elinor Ochs and Carolyn Taylor videotaped dinnertime conversations among typical middle-class families. Their research was based on more than 100 family dinner narratives. These researchers found that dinner conversations often follow a particular pattern—each person has a rigid role to play. Typically, a parent dominates the conversation, while the children feel as though their opinions do not matter or that their actions might be subject to immediate criticism. This interferes with open, meaningful, collaborative discussions. These researchers also found that family members' roles differ in the amount of power they possess.

The most powerful roles are almost always held by parents. The father, seen as the "judge," and the mother, seen as "the introducer" are higher in the familial hierarchy than the children.

Although children are often talked about and introduced by parents in dinnertime storytelling, they are rarely addressed. As a result, they sometimes feel that their opinions are not valued. The old expression "Don't speak unless you're spoken to" exemplifies this. In addition, children's actions in the stories are often critiqued by their parents. Because of this vulnerability to criticism by family members, children often do not initiate stories (especially about themselves). In general, the possibility that children feel they are under scrutiny frequently results in their resistance to storytelling. A critical part of developing new dinnertime rituals is changing the usual hierarchy of dinnertime conversations by creating a dialogue in which all family members feel equally important.

Another interesting finding was that the relationship of older to younger siblings was similar to that of parents to children. This order was apparent even in the siblings' stories. Older children controlled the story topic much more than did younger children. Hence, older siblings as well as parents are key to encouraging younger children to introduce and discuss stories.

Encouraging the involvement of the older siblings in family ceremonies is extremely important. If the younger sibling feels that the older sibling is uninterested or thinks that the ritual is silly, the younger child may take this as a cue, and as a result be much less willing to participate. In addition, parents should make sure that their older children do not pass judgment on their younger siblings. If they think they might be criticized, younger children will be less honest and imaginative in their stories.

Because the adults in the family are more experienced and more mature, they should exercise leadership in inventing more effective rituals. On the other hand, all members, including children, are more likely to feel enthusiastic about the activity if they have a hand in planning and carrying it out.

The Fine Art of Positive Response

One of the most significant ways that you can improve your family rites is to facilitate efforts to communicate well with one another. Certain kinds of responses, such as giving too much advice or pretending to have all the answers, have been shown to block the lines of communication.

For example, effective listening is more than just "not talking." It takes concentration and practice. Below are five communication skills that are useful to anyone who wants to foster good interpersonal relations in the family.

1. *Rephrase the person's comments to show you understand.* This is sometimes called "reflective listening." Reflective listening serves three purposes:

- It assures the person you hear what she or he is saying.

- It persuades the person that you correctly understand what is being said (it is sometimes a good idea to ask if your rephrasing is correct).

- It allows you a chance to reword the person's statements in ways that might be less self-critical. For example, if a person says, "Jimmy is a rotten liar!" you can say, "You feel your brother doesn't always tell the truth?" This is better, because when anyone harbors negative feelings about a family member, he also is likely to feel negatively about being a member of the family.

2. *Watch the person's face and body language.* Often a person will assure you that she does not feel sad, but a quivering chin or too-bright eyes will tell you otherwise. A person may deny feeling frightened, but if you put your fingers on his wrist, as a caring gesture, you may find that the person has a pounding pulse. When words and body language say two different things, the person's body language is usually closer to the truth.

3. *Give nonverbal support.* This may include a smile, a hug, a wink, a pat on the shoulder, nodding your head, making eye contact, or holding the person's hand (or wrist).

4. *Use the right tone of voice for what you are saying.* Remember that your voice tone communicates as clearly as your words. Make sure your tone does not come across as sarcastic or all-knowing.

5. *Use encouraging phrases* to show your interest and to keep the conversation going. Helpful phrases, spoken appropriately during pauses in the conversation, can communicate how much you care:

- "Oh, really?"

- "Tell me more about that."

- "Then what happened?"

- "That must have made you feel sad."

Remember, if you are judgmental or critical, the person may decide that you just don't understand. You cannot be a good influence on a person who won't talk to you.

Healthy Communication Practices

In summary, we turn to the bestseller, *Traits of a Healthy Family,* written by Delores Curran. In it, Curran describes her survey of 550 professionals who are currently working with families. Her study produced fifteen characteristics that are commonly perceived in the healthy family, listed in the order of the frequency with which they were mentioned:

1. Communicates and listens
2. Affirms and supports one another
3. Teaches respect for others
4. Develops a sense of trust
5. Has a sense of play and humor

6. Exhibits a sense of shared responsibility
7. Teaches a sense of right and wrong
8. Has a strong sense of family in which traditions abound
9. Has a balance of interaction among members
10. Has a shared religious core
11. Respects the privacy of one another
12. Values service to others
13. Fosters family table time and conversation
14. Shares leisure time
15. Admits to and seeks help with problems.

The number of ideas we have asked you to consider in this chapter is admittedly large. Almost certainly there are more than you can suggest to your family all at once. We hope that as you get started with ritual invention, you will pick the concepts that you believe to be most salient and practice them as a part of your activities. In time, you may want to introduce one additional concept as a part of every new rite you try. We hope that we have helped you better understand these components of the well-designed ritual, so that you can incorporate them into your own.

chapter 3

Altars and Amulets

*On an altar, the ordinary is replaced by the
extraordinary, the mundane by the magical.*

—Anonymous

The concept of the altar is an ancient one, appearing in the earliest of human writings. The word *altar* typically refers to a raised structure or place used as a focus for prayer, worship, and sometimes for sacrifice. It comes from the Latin for "high" *(alto),* probably because the original sites of worship were mountaintops, as these were deemed to be closer to the gods. Later, the sites became more specific: springs or unusual rocks that came to be esteemed as holy. Such places were often thought to be inhabited by gods or other spirits whose help was sought by worshipers. Typically, gifts to please these "inhabitants" were left on makeshift stands, such as a pile of stones, that became more elaborate with time.

Altars in ancient Israel had "horns" affixed to the four corners—anyone clinging to these horns could not be harmed. Elsewhere, altars ranged from small tables on which incense was burned to the massive constructions used in Egyptian temples. The Greeks built altars everywhere—next to the doorways and the courtyards of their houses, in their public buildings and markets, and in sacred groves. Roman altars were equally ubiquitous. Two hundred years after the crucifixion of Christ, Christians were regularly using altars in their churches to celebrate the Eucharist, the symbolic enactment of Christ's death and resurrection. Over time, their altars became quite elaborate, often containing the remains of martyrs. Their cathedrals housed numerous of these elaborate altars.

As Peg Streep explains in her resourceful book, *Altars Made Easy,*

> Separating our "spiritual" identity from other identities we have in ourlives—as workers and professionals, as wives and mothers, husbands and fathers—is also, in the scheme of history, a recent event, and a Western one at that. In most parts of the world, the ritual offering of gifts to the gods and goddesses at home and at work, at personal and public altars and shrines, is part of everyday life. Even in our Western past, the progression of life in the act of making offerings were virtually inseparable. . . . Immigrants to the United States have often brought with them traditions that connect spirituality with everyday life, only to see the later, "Americanized" generations abandon these traditions.

For our purposes, altars need not have a worshipful or religious connotation. Rather, they may be used by members of our families, believers or non-believers, as a tool to help focus attention and intention. Through designing an altar, decorating it, and placing meaningful objects on it, we can promote the same goals that we seek to achieve in our ceremonies. Altars can be one more element that we use to help our families pull together to become more joyful.

You may have an altar in your home without realizing it. Do you have a table, a mantelpiece, or perhaps a piano top on which you have arranged pictures of your favorite people? Have you put the pictures there so that you could publicly honor them as individuals and remind yourself how much you care about them? Well, if so, we would say that you have an altar. When you have people come to your house for dinner, do you sometimes decorate the dinner table with candles, flowers, and your best dishes? In a way, that too is an altar on which you will celebrate your family love or friendship for the people you have invited.

An amulet is any object that you believe has the power to help you achieve your goals. For some people, this is a charm, such as a lucky penny, a rabbit' s foot, or some other article that is associated with good fortune. Members of the Catholic and Islamic faiths often carry a set of beads in their pockets to help them deal with the stress in their lives, fingering the beads while reciting a prayer.

As with the ancient components of ceremony that we described in chapter 2, it is not necessary that you include altars or amulets in the ceremonies you design. However, we believe that if you include them, you may feel a deeper connection to the intentions of your rites. Let's examine these two concepts more closely.

Altars

Constructing and using an altar in your home means making a number of decisions: How are you likely to use it? From what materials will you make it? Will it be permanent or temporary? How will it be covered? What objects will you place on or in it? How will you light it? What scents will emanate from it? In the following sections, we suggest some answers to these questions.

The Uses of an Altar

The uses for an altar are limited only by the imaginations of the individual members of the family. Altars can:

- Focus attention on a simple idea or ideal
- Be the centerpiece for meditation
- Create a sense of wonder
- Provide spiritual comfort
- Serve as a reminder of special memories (a place for photos, for memorabilia)
- Be a place to put spiritual offerings
- Offer comfort when under stress
- Provide inspiration for problem solving
- Help eliminate negative habits and instill positive ones
- Serve as a place to record progress on a journey
- House personal treasures
- Honor ancestors
- Bring the sacred into everyday life.

Shapes

When most people think of an altar, they probably envision a flat, rectangular table. There isn't any reason that this has to be the shape, however. Even when altars are tables, they need not be rectangular. A friend of ours took a small circular table and added a semicircle to the back half, elevating it on columns about 12 inches above the table's surface. This bi-leveled altar offers a variety of possibilities; for example, our friend often puts small objects up on the semicircle level and larger objects below on the table itself. Another acquaintance installed a large wooden triangle in the corner of his bedroom at about waist level and uses that as an altar.

Altars need not be at waist level, either. Some people paint elaborate shapes on the floor or use floor tiles. Others install altars at eye level or higher so that one needs to look up in order to see what is on them. Some people prefer very simple shapes, and others favor elegant designs. It's really all up to you and your family.

You might want to study the discipline called Feng Shui. It offers an integrated system for choosing the shapes and placement of objects in a room, around a house, or in our case, on an altar. You'll find a number of books on the subject in most bookstores.

Materials Used

Altars can be constructed from a great variety of materials. You can use wooden planks, plastic, wire, metal, or cardboard. You can make an altar out of boards on bricks, a packing crate, a mirror or a thick pane of glass (which may also be hung behind the altar so that you can contemplate your own face and body as part of the ritual), a trunk, votive candles in a circle, or a large cardboard box.

You can use natural materials such as stones, cleared ground, logs laid end to end, plant leaves, tree limbs, and seashells. Small stones can be arranged in piles or in a circle or concentric circles, with each pile or circle representing a theme. It is even possible to use materials such as bricks or pebbles to create a maze or labyrinth in a yard, with an altar at the center.

Permanence

Imagine some occasion for a ceremony—it can be any kind you want. If you're going to use an altar with it, one of the decisions you need to make is how long you want to be able to keep the altar as it is. It might be that you want to use it only for that one ritual, or it could be that you want to keep it for a very long time.

Your altar might be quite temporary—used for only one ceremony. For example, it might be constructed at a campsite. You might wish it to be portable, so that it can be taken on trips. In this instance, you might want it to fit into a suitcase or briefcase. The ultimate portable altar could be as small as an amulet or folded scarf that you carry in your pocket. Even a piece of paper on which you have written or drawn symbols can serve the purpose.

Some constructions are semi-permanent—built to last but also designed so that they may be disassembled readily. Most altars, though, are probably of the permanent type—built into a special place in the house, such as the corner of a dining room or along the wall of a bedroom.

In deciding the permanence of your altar, an important consideration is whether or not you care to have others view it. If it is to be of a very personal nature, you might build an altar that is easily disassembled so that you can store it away. If you want a private altar that can be used whenever you or your family wish, you should consider putting it in a place that visitors will not have access to, such as a bedroom or an attic.

Covering

The right cover can greatly enhance the symbolic nature of the experience. An obvious choice is cloth. The cloth you use may be store-bought, hand-woven, hand-embroidered, or painted with fabric paint, preferably by the members of your family. Also usable are shawls, veils, and small rugs.

The colors of the cloth are symbolic, as can be seen on this list:

- Black for things that are scary, overcoming obstacles
- Blue for meditation, honoring someone
- Brown for death, stability
- Gold for praying to God
- Green for achievement, growth, contentment
- Orange for communication
- Pink for betrothals, renewed strength
- Purple for inspiration
- Red for passion, conflict resolution
- White for hope, purity
- Yellow for new beginnings, healing, happiness.

When cloth is used with candles, it is wise to place the candles in cups or other holders, because straight candles might drip on the cloth. The holders need not be fancy; they could just be clean aluminum cans with some holes punched in them, or juice glasses. Stones, either flat ones or pebbles, can also serve as symbolic coverings.

In ancient societies, it was believed that gods and spirits dwelled within stones, and for this reason, stones themselves were often objects of religious veneration. An example of early stone symbolism is found in the story of Jacob's dream in the Old Testament. During his travels, Jacob came to a place where he lay down to sleep. He used a stone and the ground for his pillow. During the night he had a dream that God spoke to him and offered him the land upon which he slept. In the morning, Jacob took the stone from under his head and made it a pillar, anointed it, and called the place "Beth-el." It is legend that this place later became known as Bethlehem. Other natural materials that can be used for covering include pinecones or needles, flower petals, sand, tree boughs or bark, grasses, leather, flowers, bricks, mistletoe, and corn husks.

Objects for Your Altar

In a study John conducted of the characteristics of highly effective families, it was found that virtually every family in this category had at least one collection. In most cases, the collections were of objects that were particularly meaningful, such as original editions of books written by Willa Cather, handmade Russian dolls, bottles, foreign coins, or crystals. The majority of the families had a general collection to which all members contributed, and several other collections maintained by individual members. Children seem to have a natural proclivity toward collecting. Think of all those sports cards and Beanie Babies taking up drawer or shelf space in your child's room. An altar makes an excellent place for keeping such collections, which give the family a sense of cohesion and a secure identity.

Altars can also serve as a showcase and revered location for other kinds of objects. For example, family pictures or portraits and other favorite items might be placed there, such as rings, baseball cards, statues, figurines, and other mementos. Found objects like driftwood, tree burls, shiny chestnuts, and unusual bones might be arranged on your altar, too.

Sometimes people enjoy placing purely symbolic objects on their altars. For example, they might put a mandala on it. From the Sanskrit for "circle," a mandala is a symmetrical figure, such as a circle with a cross drawn through it (for example, the Celtic cross). Mandalas may represent any theme that the maker wishes. In his excellent reference work, *The Power of Myth,* anthropologist Joseph Campbell urges readers to make their own mandalas, starting by drawing a circle and then including within it symbols of the values in their lives. We offer a similar activity, "The Family Crest," in chapter 7.

Although the Book of Genesis decreed that Adam should have dominion over animals, humans have long believed that animals are manifestations of the divine spirit. Native Americans and other pre-industrial societies commonly placed animal symbols on their altars. The animal motif is usually symbolic of human beings' instinctual nature. Many ancient myths are concerned with sacrificing the "primal" animal to the gods to appease them or to make offerings for fertility. In the religious art of almost every cultural group, animal attributes have also been ascribed to the supreme gods. The art of the Babylonians, Egyptians, and Greeks is full of animal symbolism.

Other symbolic items include representations of the four elements. For instance, feathers or pictures of butterflies or trees being blown by the spring breeze can stand for air, lotions and scented oils represent water, soil is a symbol of earth, and sunflowers, volcanic rock, rubies, or summer fruits can remind us of fire.

Scents

Another way to enhance the effectiveness of an altar is to arrange for stimulating fragrances to arise from it. The olfactory sense has a powerful effect on the emotions, and may be manipulated to bring about a wide range of feelings. Some instances of evocative aromas:

- Spices: Cloves, mustard, ginger, jasmine, juniper, pepper, mimosa

- Herbs: Tradition connotes most herbs as being symbolic of one of the four elements: Dill, lavender, marjoram, valerian (air); garlic, basil, onion, tarragon, woodruff, angelica, bay, rosemary, chamomile (fire); chickweed, poppy (water); geranium, primrose, tansy, yarrow, sage, calendula (earth).

- Oils: Lavender, citrus, eucalyptus

- Burning woods: Apple, fir, cedar

- Cooked foods: Grilled meats, stews, bread, bouillabaisse

- Incenses: Sandalwood, frankincense, white sage, pine. Not only wonderful to smell, incense produces wisps of smoke that spiral upward and have long been understood as a way of communicating with the spiritual world, as another type of prayer.

Incense is also often employed in "smudging": marking the borders of a sacred place with smoke. Native Americans typically used tobacco. They would stand in the center of the sacred place and lift their ritual pipe to the four directions, then up to Father Sky and down to Mother Earth. Smudging also has been used to mask the smells of closely packed, unwashed bodies. Participants in ceremonies sometimes sanctify themselves by using their hands to wave the smoke from an altar fire around and over their bodies. Smudges are made by binding some material such as sage into a bundle, lighting the end, and then gently blowing out the flame so that the bundle continues to produce a cloud of smoke.

Lighting

You might enhance the efficacy of your altar and add drama by the ways that you light it. Some obvious examples are the use of candles, spotlights, and Christmas tree lights.

Sounds

Finally, by incorporating sound into your altar, you add another layer of interest and depth. You have a great variety of choices that can be used to help you relax, energize yourself, or in other ways affect your mood. Rhythmic sounds are especially helpful because they assist in calming and focusing the central nervous system. Some excellent sources of sound are bells, cymbals, drums, gongs, rattles, wind chimes, and recorded chants and flute music.

Outdoor Altars

There is something special about an outdoor altar. The ground, the plants, the sky, natural light—all combine to make a backdrop that can enhance the altar's power. The purpose of an altar is to put us in touch with the miraculous; what better place to do this than in the presence of the miracle of nature?

As with indoor altars, you are faced with many options. You may build with carefully balanced stones or with stones that are cemented together. You can create a garden of flowers or vegetables or both. You can design a labyrinth with a place of worship in the center. A Zen garden, made of carefully raked sand and unadorned stones, makes an excellent choice.

John's Lily Garden

I have always loved the sound of water falling and was thinking about that one day while working in my flower garden. I remembered that my daughter had a large number of stones strewn about the woods in back of her house. I brought them to my home and piled them in the corner of my garden. I dug a large hole at the foot of the pile and lined it with plastic. In the bottom of the hole, I placed a small water pump and ran a hose from it under a layer of the rocks to the top of the pile. There I had levered several flat stones so that I could place the end of the hose out over the edge of the hole and about three feet above it. I filled the cavity with water and dropped three pots of miniature water lilies into it. Beside the little pond, I installed the carved stone face of the "Green Man," revered as a water god in Irish mythology and given to me by my friend Ralph Titus. When I plugged in the pump, a soothing stream of water splashed over the flat stones and down onto the water's surface, aerating the roots of the plants. My diminutive waterfall has encouraged the waterlilies to produce the most magnificent flowers you ever saw!

My family and I have spent many happy moments sitting beside the garden. In fact, my grandchildren might be said to worship the tiny green frogs that live there.

Amulets

An amulet is any object that is worn or carried in the hope that, in some way, it will help improve the person' s life. The concept has a very long history. The ancient Egyptians wore amulets on necklaces, and the Greeks carried protective charms called *phylakterion* with them wherever they went. These objects usually consisted of a stone or a piece of metal that had an inscription or some figures engraved on it.

Observant Jews frequently carried slips of parchment in a tiny case on which passages from the Torah were written; these were seen as protection from evil spirits and other harms. The early Christians often wore the tiny symbol of a fish, for which the Greek word is *ichthys*. This word also contains the initials of the Greek words for "Jesus Christ, Son of God, Savior."

Letters of the archaic runic alphabet used by the early Scandinavians served them as amulets. They carved individual letters into wood and stone, and carried them for symbolic protection. For example, the letter *os,* which stands for our letter *a,* was the symbol of communication, poetry, music, and the link between the gods and humanity. The letter *boerc,* our letter *b,* stands for the hope of forgiveness, atonement for misdeeds, birth, and healing. The letter *ken,* which is similar to our letters *c, k,* or *q,* relates to light and the thirst for knowledge. The person carrying one of these runes hoped to attain what the letter represented.

Today we have many words for amulets—talisman, charm, trinket, totem, sacred tool, magical object—but they all mean an object that has been blessed or otherwise empowered to accomplish some task. It has been a common practice throughout history to create amulets by placing objects on an altar and smudging them with smoke. They are also created by being blessed by a person believed to have special powers. A set of rosary beads blessed by the pope would be an example. Amulets may also be empowered through group ceremonies, as in the case of the AA medallion. Members of Alcoholics Anonymous receive a special medal each year on the anniversary of the date they stopped drinking. The presentation is made during a ceremony, and the medallion itself is embossed with Saint Francis' prayer and other meaningful symbols. Recovering alcoholics carry it with them as an aid to not take a drink. Another example would be a wedding bouquet. Because it has been carried by the bride, many believe that it takes on the power to help an unmarried woman find a suitable mate in the near future.

John's Granddaughter and Her Magic Medallion

When my granddaughter was five, her mother told me that she was becoming quite upset by thunderstorms, and asked if I could suggest a remedy. It occurred to me to select an object that might serve as an amulet to ward off her fearful feelings. I chose a brass medallion that had been given to me decades ago. She knew that it was important to me, and even though the inscription and diagram on it meant nothing to her, the medallion had the look of something special.

The next step was to consecrate it on the little altar I have built in a shed on the back of my property. The altar consists of a wooden tray affixed across a window, which contains raked sand and a few special objects that I use for meditation. We placed the medallion on the sand in the middle of the altar. Then we lit a smudge of white sage. My granddaughter waved the small smoking bundle back and forth over the medallion while I read the following words aloud:

"We are here today because we want to help this child. We want to help her not to be so afraid of the noisy thunder. The way we are going to help her is by putting magic into the special medal that is on this altar. First we're going to bless it. We want to put our strongest wishes into it so that it can protect her from being frightened. When there's a thunderstorm, we want her to pick up this medal and hold it tightly in her hand. She should realize that her whole family wants her to know that she is safe and does not have to be afraid. It will be just as though we are all there were her, putting our arms around her and protecting her from her fears. When she uses this medal, she can be certain that she will be okay."

We then took the medal to other members of the family and asked them to hold it while they said a prayer to give her courage. And it worked. During the next several storms, she used the medal, but now she really doesn't need it anymore.

chapter 4

Marking Milestones

Too often, an important event happens in a person's life—beginning kindergarten, starting to shave, entering menopause—and people pay hardly any attention to it. This is not necessarily harmful to the individual's development, but a wonderful opportunity for celebration is missed. By recognizing and celebrating these occasions through carefully designed ceremonies, the person and the family can be strengthened. Life can be made more joyful, and we can all use more of that!

ACTIVITY: The New Home

The Objective
To celebrate the transition of moving as a joyous occasion, to bring good luck to the inhabitants of the new home, and to bring warmth, caring, and the love of past homes into the new home

The Situation
Home is a very special place for most of us. Leaving a home can be traumatic for even the most transient and adventurous. In recent years, honoring a new home with a ritual has become important to

many. People in the West have become interested in the ancient Chinese practice of Feng Shui as well. Here, we describe a ceremony for a new home, whether it is a first apartment to be shared with friends or a growing family's third house in ten years. The rite is simple, because it is designed to happen at a very hectic time, within a few hours of moving, or just before moving into the new home.

Materials Needed

A Eucalyptus-scented candle for the altar, a sage smudge (available from New Age shops, health food stores, home design stores, and some stationary and bookstores), an altar cloth, and photographs of past homes. (NOTE: A sage smudge is a fist-sized bundle of dried sage, tied together with string that you light and then blow out the flame so that the bundle smokes.)

∾ ∾ ∾

It is important to give the home a thorough cleaning before moving day. After moving in, construct a temporary altar by draping a cloth over a low table or bench, or even a cardboard box if that's all that's unpacked! On the altar, place photographs of past homes, the people who were a part of your life from these homes, pets that are no longer with you, and other mementos of the past. Open all the windows in the house (unless it is truly freezing out). Burn a eucalyptus-scented candle (connotes cleansing) on the altar. With all who live in the home present, begin the ceremony at the altar with a short blessing. Then move to the room in the easternmost corner of the house, to symbolize new beginnings. With a smudge of sage and a small bowl of water, the leader of the ritual says a few words about the person who will live in that room, or about the functioning of that room. For example, in a child's bedroom one would say, "May this cozy room bring Ethan good dreams, warm thoughts, and the love of all those here today. Within these walls, may he continue to grow stronger, and happier each day." In a bathroom say something like, "May the bright morning light of this room bring each of us the joy of a new day. Help us to care for our bodies and give us the pleasure of cleanliness."

Move through each room of the house or apartment, blessing each new room in turn. Don't forget storage spaces, attics, cellars, and garages. As the speaker is doing the blessing, another person sprinkles a few drops of water from the bowl to symbolize freshness, and the sage is waved throughout the room to clear the air. (Children especially love the job of water sprinkling and sage waving.) As you leave each room, shut the window. After the whole home has been visited, regroup in the kitchen for your first meal in your new home, and rejoice!

The designated leader (and it could be anyone, including a young child) says, "Today we moved into our new home. We hope that in this home we will be blessed by our love for each other and our new friends. It is an exciting time for each of us, and we hope to have many wonderful seasons here. May we continue our journey as a family, made stronger by this new home."

ACTIVITY: Breaking Bread with the New Baby

The Objective
To celebrate a baby's birth by providing a quality meal for the new arrival and its family

The Situation
There is one thing common to all parents bringing home a new baby: being overly busy. Infants have so many needs that it's hard to take care of the everyday things. Preparing delicious meals is one of them.

Materials Needed

Cooking materials, a baby's rattle or other suitable amulet, favorite music

༄ ༄ ༄

A meal is prepared for the baby's family by the adults who care about the baby: grandparents, uncles and aunts, family friends—anyone who enjoys cooking (other than the baby's parents, who deserve a break). The baby's siblings might be involved, too. The group gathers in whoever's kitchen is best equipped and largest, perhaps on a Saturday afternoon. They discuss the menu and then go to the supermarket to buy the ingredients. They spend the rest of the afternoon preparing a sumptuous repast. Members of the group should bring their favorite music to be played while they cook. A traditional baby gift such as a rattle, perhaps one of silver or crafted by an artisan from wood, is placed in the center of the cooking area. As the cooking goes on, and if the spirit moves them, each participant picks up the rattle and offers a hope or says a prayer for the new baby's life. A tape recorder is placed near the gift to record what each person says. All of the wishes and prayers can later be typed out and put together as a keepsake for the baby.

As the cooking begins, the leader of this informal rite introduces it. Facing the East, the direction of new beginnings, she says:

"We're gathered here today in the spirit of support for [name of mother and/or father] as they begin the important task of raising [baby's name]. In addition to preparing a meal for them, we are going to imbue this rattle with the power of our prayers and hopes for little [baby's name]. As the spirit moves you, please pick up the rattle and offer your hopes and a prayer for [baby's name] future. When we are done, we will take all this food and the rattle gift over to their house and have a wonderful meal together!"

Variation

For those who enjoyed this activity and want to repeat it, perhaps on the baby's six-month birthday a similar ritual can be conducted, this time imbuing a new amulet, such as a teething ring, with the power of the group.

ACTIVITY: A New Slice of Life

The Objective

To provide guidance to a teenager on his or her fourteenth birthday

The Situation

When children reach the age of fourteen, the middle of the stage of puberty, they are in the midst of passing from childhood to adulthood. It is as though they are shedding their skin, and they are sometimes quite vulnerable. Fear stems from ignorance, so the intent of this ritual is to reduce the teenager's anxiety by sharing the experiences of others. Teens benefit when their families help to celebrate the successes and joys that are part of this stage of life.

Materials Needed

A table, chairs, plate, saucer, green cloth, pine incense, matches, a fledgling Norway pine, which will grow indoors; several pizzas

∾ ∾ ∾

The immediate family of the teenager—grandparents, parents, and older siblings, as well as close adult friends, all those who wish to participate—are present. All are seated in chairs facing a small table that serves as an altar. The rear of the altar is facing South (which symbolizes youth). The table is covered with a green cloth, an emblem of growth, and on it is a plate and a saucer. Tiny mounds of pine-scented incense are placed on the plate, one mound for each of the adults who wishes to speak. The saucer contains a small amount of incense, too. The smoke of the incense, representing the sentiments of those who speak, carries these thoughts and wishes to the heavens above. A fledgling potted Norway pine tree is in the center of the table.

If possible, the first speaker is the father of the teenager (if he is a boy) or the mother (if she is a girl), who says:

"We're gathered here today to mark an important and special occasion. [Teenager's name] is beginning the journey into adulthood. We would like to honor his/her entry into this next phase of his life, which involves many changes, both physical and emotional, positive and negative. This can be a time of wonderful adventures and great joy. However, entering into this time of life and facing these changes, even when they are for the better, can be scary. Today we want to share our experiences of what it was like for us to begin this chapter of our lives, and to give you any advice we think might help you.

"[Teenager's name], you're not alone in going through this experience. We are here to support and help you any way we can. You will not have the same experiences as we had, but we hope what we have to tell you will be of some help with this first big turning point in your life."

One by one, each of the adults lights one of the mounds of incense and tells a brief story of how they felt as an adolescent, mentioning happy as well as sad outcomes. The youth is then asked if she would be willing to say something about her hopes for the future. Before speaking, the teen lights the incense in the saucer. When done, the adults are given a chance to respond. When each of the speakers has finished, the pizzas, bubbling from the oven, are brought in. Each adult takes a piece of pizza in hand, and together they read from a sheet of paper on which these words are printed: "[Name], may your advance into adulthood bring you many adventures, and may you use each of them to grow wiser and happier." The adults then offer the teenager a hug or a handshake, and they all share the pizza together.

Variation

To celebrate the teenager's eighteenth birthday, the Norway pine that was presented at this coming-of-age ritual and that the teenager has nurtured for the past four years is taken from its pot and replanted in the earth outside. In this way it can serve as a symbol of the achievement of adulthood.

ACTIVITY: A Close Shave

The Objective:

To teach an adolescent boy the correct way to use a safety razor and to celebrate his moving into a new stage of life

The Situation

In the lives of most teenage boys, there comes a time when they feel they should start to shave. Most males learn to do it by watching our fathers or friends and proceeding by trial and error. That's the way it has been with thirteen-year-old Keiji. His father, Yutaro, could just lend him a razor and let him go at it, but it seems like this might be an opportunity to create a closer relationship between them. This ceremony is designed to be carried out by a father and his son, or some other significant adult male if the father is not present. (However, it can be easily adapted to a mother and her daughter who is learning to apply makeup or begin a similar grooming ritual.)

Materials Needed

A safety razor, shaving cream, after-shave lotion or fragrance

∿ ∿ ∿

Yutaro could give Keiji a cheap plastic razor, but he has bought his son a brass-plated razor that comes in a case. It makes the ritual they share that much more significant.

What you say to the teen will depend to some extent on how old he is. Adolescents develop secondary hair (facial, underarm, and leg hair) at differing ages; thus, how you handle this will depend on the age of the child. Yutaro points out to Keiji that he understands the young man probably already knows how to shave, but that as his father, he wants to give him some pointers on doing it well. After Keiji has lathered up, and as the shaving proceeds, Yutaro recalls aloud some of the feelings he had when he was just starting to shave. He talks about his fears, his hopes, and his dreams. Then he asks Keiji to talk a bit about his own fears and hopes.

Yutaro uses the techniques for good listening that we described in chapter 2. When the shaving has completed, Yutaro presents Keiji with a new bottle of shaving lotion—the element of water. Water is the symbol of maturity, toward which Keiji is now making a major step. Since Yutaro's gift is the same brand of after-shave that he uses, Keiji is flattered to be receiving this symbol of manhood. Then Yutaro remarks, "Well, you certainly seem to have mastered the shaving process! Let's have another talk like this sometime soon, okay? Now, how about we go out for breakfast?"

Variation

This father-son might establish a "breakfast out morning" tradition for them: they might have it at a favorite diner every Saturday morning.

ACTIVITY: New Endings and Old Beginnings

The Objective

To emotionally support and comfort the menopausal woman who might be grieving the loss of her childbearing years and may be viewing this important biological change as a symbol of her own mortality.

The Situation

Although many native cultures around the world celebrate a young woman's menarche (beginning of menstruation), few celebrate or honor the end of fertility. In this ceremony, women friends of the honoree gather to celebrate the end of her childbearing years. Usually, menopause is recognized as being complete when a woman has not had a menstrual period in one full year. Because an individual woman can experience perimenopause for as many as ten years, you may want to stage this celebration at any time during "the change."

Participating in a ritual that celebrates menopause as the beginning of a new phase of her life, instead of seeing it only as an ending, will help her to look at her future as bright and full of the wisdom of the older woman. This ceremony marks the beginning of a new phase of life, which includes a greater spiritual, psychological, and sexual freedom.

Materials Needed

Small candles (votives or Sabbath candles), one for each participant; a large candle; a large, decorative bowl; gifts from each participant; music and something to play the music on (CD or tape player)

❧ ❧ ❧

Conduct the ritual as the sun sets, indoors or out, in the autumn (symbolizing maturity). A group of women friends of the honoree gather with her in a circle and join hands. In the center of the circle on a low table, a large unlit candle sits in a decorative bowl filled with sand. Meditative music plays quietly in the background. Arranged around the bowl of sand, the four directions (and thus the four stages of life) are symbolized by a pile of seeds in the Eastern quadrant (fertility/ infancy), and a small blooming plant in the Southern quadrant (growth/youth). To the West, a ripe piece of fruit is placed (maturity/harvest), and in the Northern quadrant is a beautiful rock or polished stone (elderhood/wisdom.) Photographs of the celebrant should be included on the table or around the room.

The honoree stands with her back to the direction that symbolizes the stage of life that she is leaving (South.) Members of the group drop hands, and each is given a small candle by the eldest member of the congregation, who lights her own candle and then lights the candle of the woman to her left. The candle lighting ceremony continues this way until all the candles are lit. As each woman lights her candle, a brief wish is spoken for the honoree's future, something like, "Kathleen, I hope that the wisdom you have gained over the past years brings you confidence and joy in the years ahead."

The woman being honored then lights the large candle in the center of the circle and everyone blows out her own, smaller candle. At this point, everyone sits down and gives the honoree a gift that is intended to help her find her way in this new phase of her life. The gift could be a poem the giver wrote, an inspirational book that the giver found helpful during her own menopause, bath salts for a cleansing bath that symbolically washes away the old, allowing for the new growth. Whatever the gift, the woman giving it shares its significance with the whole group. Follow the ritual with a celebration of food and drink so that the participants can verbally share their experiences and enjoy each other's company.

The oldest woman begins with,

"Tonight, as the sun sets, we join hands to celebrate Kathleen's journey into a new and exciting phase of her life. Just as summer turns to autumn, our bodies age, too. We can each take comfort in our knowledge that with the autumn come days of glowing beauty: brilliant leaves turning red and orange and gold, the frost sparkling the grass in the early morning."

The youngest woman in the group continues by saying,

"With our growing maturity comes the wisdom of the crone, a wisdom we embrace as our time of celebration; reflection on lives well lived. Welcome, Kathleen, to the age of wisdom!"

ACTIVITY: The Wisdom of Gray

The Objective

To reexamine the excessive focus our society places on youth and celebrate the achievement of elder status

The Situation

The first gray hairs that emerge on a man are not usually welcomed. Gray hair is associated with growing old, the loss of youth and competence. Turning gray, although sometimes considered distinguished, represents a transition from youth to the middle years (autumn), if one turns gray in his forties; or from middle age to elderhood (winter), if graying later in life. It is important to dispel the notion of loss, celebrating instead the growth of a person because of the achievement of wisdom, honor, and respect. In many cultures elders are treated with reverence and are given the responsibility of being the family caretaker of tradition and lore. Yet in so many instances, contemporary America has reversed this status and made it a burden to become older.

Materials Needed

A "watersite" in the northwestern part of the yard, or, if creating an indoor rite, a fountain in the northwest corner of a room; a book of proverbs by Confucius or another philosopher; several candles; a large piece of slate and two boulders; pictures of the honored elder that depict various time periods in his life; a bottle of vintage wine, brandy, or champagne; and music, such as: "A Very Good Year" by Frank Sinatra

❧ ❧ ❧

During a late autumn weekend a family gathering takes place that includes the honoree's nuclear family and his parents and siblings, if possible. Each family member is invited to create a poem, a story, or an anecdote about the honoree. Include water in this ritual to symbolize maturity or to use as a blessing. One idea, though labor intensive, is to create a waterfall or small pool in the yard (landscape design books and software offer many plans and instructions) for the person being celebrated. Another idea is to build or buy an indoor fountain. Tabletop models can be beautiful and fairly inexpensive. The family would then gather at the "watersite." Siblings of the honoree, chosen because of their knowledge of the honoree's past, place a large piece of slate on two boulders, creating a bench that also serves as an altar. This bench would face northwesterly, overlooking the waterfall or fountain. It is important to unite the two directional symbols and elements because this is a transition from autumn to winter. The children of the honoree place pictures of the honoree, in chronological order, on the slate. A small book of proverbs is placed on the altar to honor the wisdom of the new elder. As a final presentation, a bottle of vintage wine, champagne, or brandy is opened and poured by the oldest male in the family. Each person then recites what he or she has written to toast the honoree. The spouse or partner of the person being honored gives the final toast and allows the honoree to say a few words, while a memorable song plays in the background.

Here is an introductory script you could use:

Oldest male of the family:

"The position of elder is one that is held with respect. Today we are going to recognize a new member to this group. [Name of honoree] has achieved the status of elder, a position of honor because of the wisdom he has gained throughout his stellar life. As a wine tastes better as it ages, we become more knowledgeable and appreciate what has been given to us. We too grow finer with age. Throughout [honoree's name] life we have witnessed him through our own lenses and have developed some serious and amusing episodes of his life. I now invite family members to place the slate on the two boulders to create a bench where he may sit to read a good book or to simply ponder some of life's greater questions. Each of us has prepared a short story or poem in your honor."

At closing:

"As a final toast on this wonderful autumn day, 'Our past defines what our future holds.' Your past has been one of diligence, hard work, honesty, and caring. Your future will provide our family with a trusted ear, a source for guidance, and a transcendental spot where love and nature abound. We now welcome you with a toast."

Everyone stands and toasts the honoree. Once finished, he is given time to speak.

chapter 5

Resolving Family Conflicts

Many individuals, couples, and entire families seek counseling in an effort to solve problems that arise in their relationships. While therapy is often a worthwhile avenue to consider, there is another method of problem solving we would suggest you think about: the use of ritual. We are not suggesting that ritual replace therapy, but it might be used in conjunction with therapy or before therapy is tried. The development of effective communication skills and the implementation of thoughtful ritual can greatly reduce the incidence and severity of conflict within a relationship.

ACTIVITY: Tension Treatment

The Objective
To relieve tension and thus promote a sense of closeness and cohesiveness. This is a good way to lay the groundwork for any effort at conflict resolution.

The Situation
Communication skills vary from family to family. Some families are able to verbalize their emotions to each other easily, but "opening up"

may be difficult, if not impossible, in other families. Furthermore, when family members are having a conflict, communication can further deteriorate, either by becoming more strained (that is, distant, cold, or dismissive), or more heated (that is, insulting or condescending). Most often, this is because everyone feels tense, especially those directly involved in the conflict, and their thinking tends to be rigidified by that tension (see chapter 2). For these reasons, a ritual that does not rely on language or a script can help to relieve everyone's anxieties.

Materials Needed

Bowl with a small amount of cedar or mesquite chips, matches

ख़ ख़ ख़

First, light a small pile of cedar or mesquite chips in a bowl, then blow out the flame so that the soothing scent permeates the room. All members of the family stand in a circle and close their eyes.

The ritual leader introduces this activity by saying,

"We have come together today to help [participants' names] resolve their conflict. Before we start that process, though, let us perform a brief ritual to help us all be in the best possible mental state to achieve that goal."

Instruct participants to turn to their left, and, with their eyes closed, begin massaging the shoulders of the person in front of them. This continues for one minute, with no speaking (pleasurable groans are allowed, however!). Then everyone turns around and massages the shoulders of the person who has just massaged them. Finally, all turn left to face the center of the circle; their eyes still closed. They hold hands, remaining silent breathing deeply, for about two more minutes.

Through this physical activity, participants will be better able to reflect upon their feelings for each other rather than verbalizing or censoring their emotions. While this may feel a bit odd at first, especially in families in which touching each other is rare, eventually members will become habituated to it and may want to use this approach for many other types of ritual. Ideally, the sense of physical closeness will serve to decrease the amount of tension felt in the family and promote a more satisfactory resolution of the problem.

ACTIVITY: What I Like about You

The Objective
To help children express positive feelings about one another after they have resolved an argument, but still feel somewhat angry at each other.

The Situation
When it comes to their siblings, many times it is easy for children to emphasize the bad behavior over the good. Even after an argument appears to have been settled, some hurt feelings are likely to remain; memories of name-calling can continue to be painful.

Materials Needed
Paper, pen, a bowl, a glass of water, a small hand towel

ৡ ৡ ৡ

Let's assume your children have just resolved some conflict, such as a disagreement about who started a screaming match. They agree that they were both responsible, but that hasn't erased the damage to the relationship.

Instruct each of the participants (there may be more than two) to go to separate spaces where they each feel comfortable. Ask them to write on a piece of paper the following statement: "In the past month, I saw you [the person with whom they have the conflict] do [some behavior that I liked], and I liked it because [reasons]." They describe at least three positive things they have admired recently about the other person. The statements should be exchanged in the evening before bedtime. This way the day ends on a happy note. The children take turns reading aloud what their siblings have written about them and making any comments that they like. When finished, each writer places a bowl on a surface under the hands of the sibling she has written about and pours part of a glass of water over the hands. As each performs this service, they say the following words:

"I hope that through these written words, any pain you have caused each other might be erased, any hurtful comments forgotten, and your true feelings about each other conveyed. Now pour the water for each other, and let us hope that you can wash your hands of this whole matter."

When done, the pourer provides a towel for hand drying. This procedure is repeated by each sibling who has written a statement. This ritual represents the real end of their argument.

Variation

It is important that this procedure not be overdone. There are only so many positive behaviors that can be cited before the exercise begins to become repetitive (and thus less sincere). This ritual should be repeated only as a resolution to major altercations. When you do repeat it, the statements may be varied. For example, instead of "In the past month, I saw you do [X], and I liked it because [Y]," the instruction could be, "In the past month, I learned [X] from you," or "I was thinking about you and it occurred to me that . . . ."

ACTIVITY: State of the Family Meeting

The Objective

To get some control back in our busy lives by planning ahead and dreaming together again.

The Situation

This activity, which Lynne's family uses, is one for *preventing* conflict! After our first son was born, my husband and I, like so many other new parents, were astounded at how little time we had for just the two of us. We felt overwhelmed by this tiny little boy who was so time consuming. We always seemed to be reacting to the unexpected new tasks that we faced each day. All our previous dreams seemed to drift away as we struggled just to maintain in the day-to-day reality of new parenthood. We made a dedicated effort to go out together at least once every month, but also began having an annual planning time together. We dubbed this time together our "Annual State of the Family Meeting."

❧ ❧ ❧

Plan ahead so that you can find a babysitter, if needed, and gather the materials so that you don't spend your precious planning time running around looking for supplies. Either have the sitter take the children out for several hours, or plan to leave the home for that same amount of time.

We hold this meeting in January, because that is the New Year, and write down a loose agenda several weeks in advance so that we have some focus. You may want to have your planning celebration at a different time, such as the anniversary of your first kiss, your wedding anniversary, or Rosh Hashanah, the Jewish New Year.

Hold the meeting at a special place where you can converse freely without interruption. Don't answer the phone, don't go to a café where your friends might join you. You may want to curl up on the couch together or go for a walk in the park, sitting under a favorite shade tree for writing time.

We begin our meeting by stating affirmations about our relationship, such as, "Together we are building a strong family." Or, "We are resourceful and creative in our daily lives together." Even though we may not feel especially strong at that moment, an affirmation states our commitment to a strong future.

Then we talk freely about our hopes and disappointments, pleasures that the previous year has brought us, and our fears about the future. If the ritual is done in the evening, we include candles, sometimes lighting a candle for each affirmation. A relaxing atmosphere is vital, so be sure to build in the components that relax the two of you.

When we are ready, we move into the more formal aspect of the ritual, following our previously prepared agenda and writing down our thoughts and responses. It is good to keep a notebook for reference that holds several years of notes from these annual meetings. We are always amazed at what we accomplished in previous years and how much more we still want to do. Reviewing the past has helped us be more realistic in our planning. Our agenda follows, but you may change it to reflect what is important to your family:

- Review of the previous year
- Personal goals for each of us for the upcoming year
- Couple's goals (what we can do to strengthen our bond/ commitment to each other)

- Family goals (what we can do to strengthen our family's bond; special issues we need to be thinking about in parenting or in caring for members of our extended family)
- House and yard plans
- Family outings and vacations we'd like to take
- Financial planning
- Long-term goals or projects we'd like to think about.

At the close of our time together, we reflect silently on our lives and leave our meeting transformed; we are a new couple!

Variation

We have learned that follow-up is essential. We eventually began scheduling seasonal meetings as a follow-up to our January "State of the Family Meeting." The seasonal meetings have grown, over the course of fourteen years, into a night away from home for my husband and me. We take our family meeting notebook and check in on the ideas we spoke of in January. We always go to the same inns, as this is viewed as comfort time for us, not adventure time. We go away to nurture each other and our dreams as a couple. This overnight is as refreshing as weeks away, and we look forward to our time together for months.

ACTIVITY: The Peace Zone

The Objective

To resolve a conflict in a rational, fair way that leaves the participants with the feeling that they have been heard and that what they have to say matters.

The Situation

Often when people are arguing, their emotions run away with them. Adrenaline floods their veins and they become angrier. The anger fuels the response and creates a vicious cycle of emotive responses driving autonomic responses and vice versa. In this state, it is difficult to really listen to what the other person is saying, as anger clouds our ability to hear. A small quibble can blow up into a full-blown fight, after which neither person can remember what the argument was initially about. The purpose of this ritual is to curb the physiological responses that lead to negative behaviors, to slow a burgeoning argument, and to impel the participants to step back and cool down. Only then can they give the situation a more objective, rational look.

Materials Needed

Comfy place where everyone can sit, chamomile, passionflower, "Sleepytime" or some other tea, hot chocolate (preferably decaf) or warm milk; lavender or other relaxing-scented oil; Peace Zone Form, printed or photocopied in advance

• • •

Prepare a "Peace Zone," that is, a relaxing location where the family can sit at similar levels so no one feels dominated by anyone. A floor with comfortable spots for people to sit works well. The Peace Zone is a place that is easily available during times of need. It includes an herb-scented oil in a vessel that can be heated to produce an aroma with a tranquilizing effect (lavender and wintergreen are two good examples). The vessel, usually a metal pot purchased in a health food store, comes on a stand under which a votive candle is inserted. A soothing, easy-to-prepare beverage such as herbal tea (not liquor) is also readily available for the occasion.

According to the principles of Feng Shui, the shape and colors of objects (see chapter 3) in one's surroundings will affect the flow of *chi*, the energy force that circles around and through us. Round, undulating, or wavy shapes and pastel blue and green colors tend to make the chi (effect of the place) more engaging, creating sensations of relaxation and warmth in a room. Round objects (votive candles, round cushions or pillows, beanbag chairs) are also good choices.

As soon as possible after a conflict between or among family members erupts, any member may convene the family to the peace zone to attempt a resolution. Someone prepares the tea and lights the oil warmer. When everyone is comfortable, each person involved fills out the Peace Zone Form that has been prepared in advance—a fill-in-the-blank form that has four phrases and corresponding spaces to write:

1. To me, this argument is about _____.

2. I think that [the other person] thinks this argument is about _____.

3. This situation makes me feel _____.

4. A fair way of solving this problem might be _____.

Next, read the following statement:

"We are gathered as a family to solve a problem. We love and respect each other very much and promise to abide by the two very important Peace Zone rules: First, each person has a chance to read his complete response to the Form before anyone else may reply. Second, after each person involved in the conflict has read her or his statement, all will get a chance to make whatever points desired. We promise to work very hard until this problem is resolved because we love each other very much. Our family is strong, and when we work together, we can handle any challenge that comes our way."

Everyone who is involved in the conflict reads a response to the questions on the Peace Zone Form and a discussion about what each person wrote follows. You may want to use a talking stick for this part of the ritual (can be an ordinary or decorated stick, a bean bag, or any small object). No one may speak unless handed the talking stick by the previous speaker.

If a resolution can be reached, then the family burns the sheets (in the sink, outside, wherever it is convenient) and a group hug follows. If a resolution cannot be reached that evening, each holds on to his sheet, and all promise to consider what they have heard that evening and to reconvene as soon as possible.

ACTIVITY: We Didn't Divorce Our Kids

The Objective
To acknowledge the continued commitment that each partner in a divorced couple has made to the children in the family

The Situation
Many couples who have ended their marriages in divorce are still committed to raising their children in the loving, nurturing way that they did when married. They didn't divorce the children, after all—only each other. In the struggle to adjust to the new arrangements, sometimes this is forgotten. It requires a great deal of maturity to be able to participate in this kind of ceremony, so it may need to happen several years after the divorce takes place. However, it is a healing rite, and we think you will find that everyone benefits—the parents, the children, the extended family, new spouses and stepsiblings as well.

Materials Needed
A bouquet of fresh flowers for the altar or front of the sanctuary,

music of the family's choice for beginning and ending of ceremony, prepared script for the clergy person and family members

∋ ∋ ∋

If your faith community would honor such a ceremony, try to conduct this ritual in its sanctuary, with an affiliated clergy person officiating. It is very important that the children help you write this ceremony and are a vital part of it. Consider inviting stepparents, step- and half-siblings, extended family, and close family friends.

Have a bouquet of your children's favorite flowers (or flowers in their favorite colors) in the front of the assembly. Choose a song to be played or sung as you walk in from the back. A lullaby or favorite hymn or folksong is perfect. Walk in as a family if the aisle width permits. The children should be in the middle with a parent on either side. When you reach the front of the sanctuary, stand in a semicircle facing the gathered guests, again with the children in the middle of the grouping. The clergy person should stand slightly at an angle so that her or his back is not turned on anyone directly.

The clergy person then leads the service by introducing the family, and saying,

> *"Today we join Rachel and Joel as they reaffirm their commitment to their children, Amy, Michael, and Josh. Although their marriage did not continue as they had hoped, and despite working very hard at making their relationship loving, they were divorced two years ago. Since then, Joel and Rachel and the children have been sharing their lives in a loving, thoughtful, caring way. Joel and Rachel live only a few miles from each other, are active in the children's schools and religious school, and divide their time with the children as equally as is possible. They are committed to raising their children in a stable environment, with two nurturing parents."*

The clergy person continues by asking for the prepared statements of the family:

> *"Each of the family members has prepared a brief statement that they would like to share with us all. Amy, would you please begin?"*

Then Amy (age twelve) would proceed with her statement, a short and amusing poem she wrote about the differences between her mom's home and her dad's. After each child has had a turn, the parents read what they have written.

Joel has written a particularly moving piece about how painful the divorce was for him. He speaks of the difficulty of getting beyond his anger, but that in the end, Rachel has helped him through her understanding and patience. He says that Rachel is a wonderful mother and that he now feels that he and Rachel are friends, working together in the most important roles of their lives.

The extended family rise from their seats to show their shared love and support of the family. While still standing, the clergy person asks for a unison reading about the importance of community in raising children; not only the children of this family, but of every family. The family then leaves down the center aisle, again to music.

ACTIVITY: I Will Survive

The Objective
To learn to let go of pain through self-nurturing.

The Situation
There are times in our lives when the pain of a relationship seems too much to bear. Whether it is a chronic argument that no one ever seems to win, angry, hateful words exchanged without thinking, or some

equally devastating scenario, sometimes we must recognize that we may have done all we can for the moment and forgive ourselves. This ritual is for individuals but, if it benefits that one person, the whole family is helped.

Materials Needed
Bath salts or gel, a pen and some paper, a receptacle suitable for burning paper

✿ ✿ ✿

For this ritual, choose a day when you can be home alone (or somewhere else) with no one to bother you. Taking the whole day to yourself is ideal, but if that is not possible, then make sure you have at least a few hours to yourself.

Wake late, turn off the telephone, don't check your e-mail, leave the radio and television off, eschew communication with the world. Begin your day by taking note of the weather and thanking the universe for yet another day, no matter how gloomy it may be. Draw a bath and pour into it revitalizing salts or bath gel. (A citrus scent is known for its energizing qualities.) In your bath, let your thoughts wander. Do not try to focus on anything in particular other than the sound of your own heartbeat and your breathing. Relax. Let the worries and past exhaustion float away. Feel yourself being completely cleansed, inside and out. Repeat affirmations such as, "I am loved by myself, my family and friends. I am clean and pure. I feel the anger of yesterday leaving my being as I wash myself." When you feel relaxed, use a wet loofah to thoroughly scrub your skin.

After the bath, prepare your favorite light breakfast. Keep silence during your meal. Just be. Again, let your thoughts drift wherever they may go.

When the meal is over, get out a pen and some paper and begin describing all the feelings that you remember from the incident that bothers you. Don't worry if the sentences aren't complete, or if it doesn't make sense. Writing single words is fine, too. Let the writing take as long as it needs.

When you are finished, and you may feel quite drained after this exercise, read what you have written. If you think someone you care about may be very hurt by your words, or you are ashamed of them, crumple up the paper, put it in a coffee can, the fireplace, or somewhere else where you can burn them safely.

Now it is time for a long walk. This isn't meant as exercise, so don't try to speed walk or count it as your aerobic workout for the day. The walk is simply meant to let you be outdoors, in a different environment. Walk for at least an hour, without intention. Don't walk to the grocery store or to a friend's house. Try to walk in a park or in a relatively private place that you enjoy.

When you return home, ease yourself into the remainder of the day by listening to music, calling a friend you haven't seen in a long time, or reading the newspaper. Continue to be gentle to yourself, but allow the distractions of the world to re-enter your day slowly.

chapter 6

Recognizing Your Family's Cultural and Religious Heritage

E very family, no matter how it is composed, has a cultural heritage. In most cases, it also has a history of religious affiliation. In recent decades, however, our society has become much more diverse, primarily because members of different backgrounds have intermarried. As a result, there has been a tendency to pay less attention to two factors that used to be of great importance to the family: culture and religion.

This is understandable, of course, but we pay a price for the trend. Cultural and religious customs can be powerful aids when the going gets rough. Further, to the extent that a family is able to recognize and agree on the religious and cultural heritage it shares, that family is likely to be more cohesive. Therefore, in this chapter, we provide activities aimed at helping your family achieve these desirable goals.

ACTIVITY: Memory Diary

The Objective

To create a history that outlines the day-to-day happenings of our lives.

The Situation

So much of our lives are lived unconsciously. We move through our days doing mundane but necessary tasks. We forget that as we live, our family histories are being created. The stories we beg our elders to tell us about their lives seem so rich compared to our own lives; yet, their stories are history they created, often while doing the same repetitive work that we do now. How will we remember the little things that don't seem very monumental now but are the fabric of future tales?

Materials Needed

Blank journal or materials for making one, family calendar, pen or pencil, decorating supplies (optional)

∿ ∿ ∿

Purchase, or make, if you are ambitious, a large blank journal (8½" × 11" is a nice size). Although anyone in the family can record events in the journal, it might be best if one person is the designated "recording secretary."

Make it a habit to quickly jot on the family calendar an event at the time it happens. Things you may want to note are the first snowfall in a new house, the first time a child carves her own pumpkin, a swimming level achieved, orthodontia applied or removed, or a new job.

Once a month, sit down with the family calendar in hand and write in the journal all the things that happened in the previous month, with dates noted. It is a record of beginnings and endings, a place to document some of the little riches that make your family different from any other. You may decide to decorate the cover of your family journal.

Some descriptions that are written in the Weygint family journal include the camping trip last summer that included eleven days of rain (we felt like heroes); Mom's record-length splinter from the same camping adventure; the death of a beloved pet; the first and last days of school; the first time one son swam the butterfly stroke; another son's hat trick during a hockey game, and so on.

At the end of the year (New Year's Eve is a great time to do this ritual), sit down with your family and read through the previous year's entries. Have a different person read each month to give it a little variety. You will be amazed at how many of the "little" things you have forgotten. The memories will start the stories that will live through the ages.

"Remember that summer when it rained for our *whole* camping trip?"

"Yeah, and we read all 734 pages of *Harry Potter and the Goblet of Fire!*"

"That is my favorite book in the whole world."

"Mom still talks about that splinter under her toenail!"

"Oh, and Jamie learned how to play Crazy Eights and has never lost a game since!"

"That was the best vacation, wasn't it? It didn't really matter that it rained so much."

The story has begun and will be embellished over the years so that great-grandchildren may hear of a camping trip with forty days of rain; a brave, brave soul who withstood the agonies of the biggest splinter known to man; cozy hours in the tent reading a classic tale;

and a card game that every child in the lineage now knows, thanks to Jamie. This is how history is made: one small tale at a time.

ACTIVITY: Food Roots

The Objective
To preserve the family's heritage by recording its favorite foods and stories.

The Situation
Many elderly folks fondly reminisce about the past, commonly known as the "good ol' days." Whether the economy in those earlier times was in a boom or a bust, they regularly gathered with others in their extended family.

As a youngster, Maria can recall many of her family holidays spent at her grandparents' home with her aunts and uncles, drinking, singing, and eating her grandmother's wonderful Italian cooking. It was common for the talk to switch to the past and to change into the family's native tongue. Her grandparents are now gone, and the whole family no longer gathers. That's why Maria has decided to try and capture the family's cultural identity through recording its techniques of cooking as well as sharing some of its stories.

Materials Needed
Ingredients for the meal, video recorder, videotape

     ❧ ❧ ❧

When possible, Maria organizes a time when one of the elders in her extended family is able to come to her house and teach her and her family how to make a traditional Italian dish. As the preparation of the dish is going on, one of the family members videotapes the event. Maria makes sure that the cook carefully describes the ingredients as well as the technique.

Someone is assigned to describe from where in Italy the recipe originates and who in the family is best known for making the dish. The same person is responsible for telling a humorous or favorite family story. This can include information about where the family grew up, what life was like then, what family gatherings were like, or how some traditions may have started. This, too, is videotaped. Once the meal is prepared, Maria's family, together with the guest cook, sit to enjoy the dinner and continue the conversation.

The meal is always opened with the following statement: "We are thankful for the time that we have spent together preparing this dinner, and for the opportunity to gain a greater understanding of our family's heritage. As we grow older, it is our responsibility to record and pass on our family's cooking techniques and traditions to the new generations. We want them to understand why we cook as we do, where we came from, and what our family history is."

Variation

Once some of these cooking sessions are recorded on video, a "family tree" of short clips of stories can be completed. Also, Maria's nuclear family might create their own dishes to be passed down.

ACTIVITY: A Cultural Heritage Hunt

The Objective

To learn about the cultures that makes your family who you are today. One of the ideas behind this is to involve the children in both current family life and to learn about their origins.

The Situation

America is a country primarily of immigrants, some of us arriving centuries ago, others arriving quite recently. Most of us are a mix of several cultures and don't necessarily have a strong sense of a single cultural identity. How did your family make the trip to America? Where did they come from and why did they come? What other questions interest you and your family about your unique history?

Materials Needed

Paper, pencils, whiteboard, crayons, maps, family heirlooms, books, photo albums

            ৠ   ৠ   ৠ

A specific day each month is designated as family heritage day. On this day, the family joins together to carry out a specific heritage-learning experience.

The family starts by spending one afternoon in a brainstorming session, listing all the relatives they know. Using a photo album may make it easier. Take this list and draw a rough family tree (or two—one for the father's family and one for the mother's), showing who is related to whom, where they live, birthdays, ages, and so on.

During the next month's family heritage meeting, the family reviews the family tree, perhaps discussing how the different people in the family came to be where they are, beginning with the history of their own immediate family. For example, if an uncle has moved away, explain that the he left home for college, then found a job in a different city, married, and decided to stay in that city. A map can be used to show where relatives have moved.

During a subsequent family heritage meeting, invite a relative to come and speak about how they came to be where they are today. For example, grandparents can explain how their great-grandparents came from Europe to find "the American dream" and started working in a factory before founding their own company. They can talk about both the hardships and the old way of life, and share family heirlooms. (Recording the stories for future reference is a good way to be certain all the details are accurate.) The family may then drive around the city and show the children where their parents and grandparents used to live and attended school.

Variation

Have the children create a book or journal documenting the family's discussions and outings. This gives them something to look forward to, and in the end they have a family reference guide, with pictures, information, and maps. As the children grow older, they may transfer the information into a computer program, creating a database of family members, scanning in recent pictures of relatives. The book can become an heirloom. This could ultimately lead to a family reunion as well, or a trip to the family's countries of origin.

ACTIVITY: Our Own Holiday

The Objective

To foster a sense of unique group identity within your family.

The Situation

We all celebrate holidays that we identify with our cultural heritage or religion. The traditional rituals that accompany such holidays are often so widely prescribed or dictated through organized religious practice (lighting the Menorah at Hanukkah, wearing green on St. Patrick's Day, fasting for Ramadan), that an individual family either cannot or would not dare to change or radically personalize them (especially when other extended family is involved). For this reason, it is beneficial and fun for a family to adopt their own holiday, which they have full liberty to modify and personalize in whatever way they wish.

Materials Needed

This depends on the ritual you choose with your family. In the first scenario following, the family would need a photo of the great-grand-parents, and other supplies to support their choices.

This new holiday could range from serious to lighthearted. You may want to celebrate Ground Hog Day, the first snowfall, the summer solstice, May Day, or the birthday of a philosopher or author you admire. Decide which holiday to adopt as your own, then choose specific elements of celebration that will be included as part of the new holiday.

Let's say that your family chooses January 29 for their special family holiday. Not only is January 29 National Puzzle Day, but it also happens to commemorate the day that the children's great-grand-parents were married in 1911. By honoring the wedding day of the great-grandparents, the family is in essence creating a tribute to their ancestors, whom they may or may not have known well. Such a choice of holiday might emphasize the importance of one's heritage or personal history. In this example, if your family has the time and financial resources for it, you could take an old picture of the great-grandparents to a photo shop and have a jigsaw puzzle cut from a reproduction. Then, family members gather around and work on the puzzle as one of the group activities. Include foods you all love, and a celebration is born!

One family we know always celebrates the first snowfall with a "personal day." The entire family stays home from school or work and enjoys the coming of winter. Even if the snow amounts to just a few stray flakes, or turns quickly to rain, this family has cocoa, plays board games, and rents a video. You may not feel that your family can responsibly stay home without a "legitimate" excuse, so celebrate the first snow the following Saturday.

ACTIVITY: Researching Your Religion

The Objective
To encourage the family to study its religious beliefs and to come to share these beliefs to the fullest extent possible.

The Situation
Thirty years ago, over 90 percent of Americans reported belonging to an organized religion. Although the figure is nearly as high today, we participate in our religious practices with less loyalty and reliability. Further, we know considerably less about our religions and their tenets than people did thirty years ago. Whatever your attitude toward religious practice, you can be assured that the family that agrees on its religious views is more likely to have cohesive relationships.

Materials Needed
Book about the family's religion, polished stones, plate, small board

         ᴂ ᴂ ᴂ

In this ritual, the family gathers to learn more about the history and tenets of its religion. The activity might take place on Sunday mornings, possibly before attending religious services. In the week preceding the meeting, on a rotating basis, a member of the family goes to the library and chooses a book that explains some aspect of the family's faith. Some examples:

- *The End of Days: Fundamentalism and the Struggle for the Temple Mount* by Gershom Gorenberg
- *A Fire in the Bones: Reflections on African-American Religious History* by Albert J. Raboteau
- *Surprised by Truth: 11 Converts Give the Biblical and Historical Reasons for Becoming Catholic* by Patrick Madrid
- *Understanding the Times: The Religious Worldviews of Our Day and the Search for Truth* by David A. Noebel

The person selects a brief passage from the book that will be understandable to the members of the family who are old enough to comprehend basic religious concepts.

Prior to the ritual, the book is placed on the family's altar, which can be as simple as a board set on the backs of two chairs. On a plate next to the book, a set of polished stones is placed, one stone for each member who will be attending. You can get a bag of such stones inexpensively at a hobby shop. The person who selected the reading should now read from the book while placing one hand on top of the stones.

The reader introduces the reading with the following statement:

"As I read the following selection, may the wisdom in the words in this book be passed through my hand and into these stones. May our discussion afterward further empower them with our love and caring for each other. As we carry these stone amulets in our pockets for the coming week, may they help us find the strength of our religious faith and of our mutual desire to be strong and wise in all our endeavors."

When the reading is finished, the reader passes the plate around to the other members of the family, allowing them to select the stone of their choice. For the next forty-five minutes, family members share their reactions to the reading, perhaps stating which parts they especially liked or would like to explore further.

Variation

If you decide that you like this use of a polished stone as an amulet for your family rituals, you might wish to purchase a stone-polishing machine. You could use it to polish stones that the family collects for itself.

ACTIVITY: How Religion Can Help

The Objective

To improve a family's understanding of its shared religious beliefs, and especially to enhance its awareness of how religion can be of assistance when the whole family is suffering.

The Situation

In 1975, Mark's mother was diagnosed with multiple sclerosis. Since the time of her diagnosis, the disease has disabled her to the point where she is bedridden, her speech is limited, and she is fed through a feeding tube. Recently, Mark's father called his two sons. He informed them that he didn't think just visiting their mom in the hospital was adequate anymore. The pain of it was becoming too great. He thought the whole family needed some spiritual help, Mom included, and wondered whether the two boys felt the same.

They agreed that they did. Mark suggested that perhaps their family's religion could be of more help. As a result, the sons and their father realized that they all needed a much better understanding of their shared religious beliefs, especially what their religion had to say about suffering. They decided to involve Mark's mother in the search for help, and with her assistance, designed a weekly ritual to help them achieve this.

Materials Needed

A carved crystal, a CD of inspirational music, a CD player

കൾ കൾ കൾ

Once a week, Mark's family gathers around his mother's bedside. Lovingly, one of the brothers places a beautiful crystal in her hand. The crystal is an earth symbol of the darkness that has engulfed the family, but the light transmitted through the crystal gives a promise of hope. Through their use of it, the crystal has become a powerful amulet.

Inspirational music is played softly on a portable CD player. The ritual begins with a family prayer led by a different family member each week. An example of prayer that Mark offered is, "Thank you, Lord, for allowing us the opportunity to spend time with our loved ones. We understand that there is wisdom greater than our comprehension that allows us to remain a family, both in this life and the next. We cherish the time that we can spend here. Please help us now to reach a greater understanding of the beliefs that we share in common, and a tolerance of those on which we disagree."

Next, some time is spent sharing a reading found by one of the sons, who have taken on the task of researching the tenets of the family religion. The readings come from various sources: the Bible, their church's weekly newsletter, books recommended by their pastor, and an article from a newspaper or magazine that has to do with religious values.

The son who does the reading explains the central point and states a personal position on it. The others then state their views, and whoever introduced the reading offers a summary of the parts where they all agree and where there is disagreement. Although the boys' mother is unable to contribute much to the discussion, they can see from the gleam in her eyes that this experience is one she cherishes.

Variation

In many nursing homes, there are seasonal fairs (fall crafts fairs and Christmas fairs, for instance) that usually are in desperate need of assistance. In keeping with their beliefs, Mark's family helps, both monetarily and physically, with the Christmas fair at his mother's nursing home. Each family member chips in to purchase food, and then they organize the kitchen for the fair. This activity helps them feel they are practicing their religion as well as reading about it.

chapter 7

Clarifying Personal and Family Values

Most of us have at least some idea of what our personal values are and what our families stand for. But how often do we discuss these values with each other in a family setting? How often do we articulate our values even to ourselves? If someone asked you right now about the values of the family you grew up in, would you be able to answer easily? Do you feel confident that your children could answer easily, too?

Sitting down and talking about the things that matter to your family is one way of teaching about values. In this chapter, we offer exercises for expressing, teaching, and learning values. Once you are able to identify and communicate your values, you will be better able to live them.

ACTIVITY: Personal Shield

The Objective

To provide an opportunity for family members to clarify their own deepest personal values by helping them understand what they most like to do.

The Situation

If our families are to have a solid, agreed-upon set of values, the individuals in them need to have a clear sense of their own values. Before that can happen, it is essential that they be aware of the kinds of activities they most like to do and why.

Materials Needed

Copies of the Things I Like to Do and My Personal Shield forms

∽ ∽ ∽

At their convenience, but before a family meeting, members fill out the Things I Like to Do form below. They list twelve of their favorite activities in the first column, and then insert the ratings called for in the instructions that follow. (Younger children will need help with this.)

Things I Like to Do

12 Things I Like to Do	$	A/P	PL	N5	I	R	M	U	C	1-5
1										
2										
3										
4										
5										
6										
7										
8										
9										
10										
11										
12										

In the columns following each activity, mark with an *x* the symbols that apply:

$\qquad$ $ $\qquad$ An activity that costs more than $7

A/P $\qquad$ An activity that is usually done alone *(A)* or is usually done with other people *(P)*

PL $\qquad$ An activity that requires planning ahead

N5 $\qquad$ An activity that would not have been listed five years ago

I $\qquad$ An activity that involves intimacy

R $\qquad$ An activity that has an element of risk

M $\qquad$ An activity that you would not mind telling your mother about

U $\qquad$ An activity that other people would say was unconventional

C $\qquad$ An activity that you hope your children will also do someday

1-5 $\qquad$ Finally, indicate your five favorite activities in order, with 1 being your most favorite.

When they have finished filling out this form, family members gather together and look for patterns. They ask themselves questions such as, "Do the ratings from 1 to 5 seem to match with other categories, such as how much the activity costs?" "Am I unwilling to let my mother know about most of my activities?"

Next, they think about what these choices say about their values in life. What really matters to them? Are they thrifty or do they like to spend money? Are they risk takers? Are they altruistic (concerned about the needs of others)? Are they something of a loner and like to be left alone? What in general is their relationship to their fellow human beings? The family compares the columns and discusses each person's patterns.

Then, working individually again, they use their conclusions about their values to create their Personal Shields. Each participating family member will make one. For this task, they use symbols instead of words. Each person creates five symbols to represent each of their five most important values, the ones of which they are the most proud. For example, if they value thinking creatively, they might use a drawing of a light bulb over a head to symbolize the concept. Here's how to complete the Personal Shield

1. In the number 1 space, draw a symbol of the value of which you are most proud.

2. In the number 2 space, draw a symbol of the value of which you are second most proud.

3. In the number 3 space, draw a symbol of the value of which you are third most proud.

4. In the number 4 space, draw a symbol of the value of which you are fourth most proud.

5. In the number 5 space, draw a symbol of the value of which you are fifth most proud.

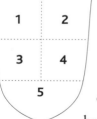

PERSONAL SHIELD

When everyone's shield is done, the family gathers in the attic, cellar, or another room in which they don't ordinarily meet. Why there? Because they're trying to break free from stereotypes and get to those values they and their family most believe in. Meeting in a room they have probably never used as a group might help. They fill a bowl with hot water and add a few drops of rose oil for inspiration. By turns, each person shares the most interesting things they learned about themselves from the Things I Like to Do form. Then each person passes around the shield he or she produced to see if the others can guess what the symbols mean. Finally, everyone states their reactions to what each shield reveals.

ACTIVITY: Family Crest

The Objective
To help the family create a family crest that can help move them toward a clearer picture of the shared values that bind them together.

The Situation
Most families have a difficult time identifying their shared values; it's just not something we talk about much. The clarification of individual values (the goal of the Personal Shield activity) can be a helpful stepping stone to identifying those common values the family most strongly holds. Ideally, the Family Crest activity should be built on the Personal Shield activity and might immediately follow it.

Materials Needed
Six 3" × 5" cards for each participant, a large bowl, material for producing a family crest, such as a piece of cardboard

෴ ෴ ෴

As with the previous activity, hold this one in the attic, cellar, or other room not regularly used as a group, someplace that is likely to inspire fresh thinking about the family's values. Have the group sit facing North, the direction that fosters wisdom. Provide each member of the family with six 3" × 5" cards. On each of the cards each family member prints a sentence that they would like to see as one of the family's central values. Examples of sentences they might write:

- We are deeply committed to each other.

- We help each other out.

- We have a lot of fun with each other.

- We are strong financially.

- We are helpful to others in need.

As each card is completed, it is dropped into a large bowl placed in the center of the group until all of the cards are in the bowl. Then, as a group, go through the cards and sort them into piles according to the category of value that they represent. For example, "We help others in need" and "We lend a hand to a neighbor" could go in the same pile. The three piles that have the most cards in them are considered, for the purposes of this exercise, to represent the family's three most important values. They might, for instance, involve loyalty to each other, honesty, and fairness and service to others, with each value defined in terms of how the family will act on it.

One of the family members should draw a crest, similar to the Personal Shield, except without the numbers and lines. The crest could be made out of thick cardboard. If a more permanent product is desired, someone might saw a crest out of a piece of good wood. Another person might like to look up the word *crest* in the dictionary to get an idea of what a family crest looks like. Typically, a family crest displays three symbols that represent what the family stands for. To make such a crest, a family needs to discuss and agree on the symbols that represent the three values they chose. For instance, if one of the family's values is a willingness to be helpful to friends and neighbors in trouble, the symbol might be one hand reaching out to another.

After they determine the symbols to be used, they decide what colors they should be. For example, blue might stand for strength and courage, green for adventurousness and creativity, and yellow for supportiveness (see the chart on the symbolic meaning of colors in chapter 3). Be aware, however, that there is no general rule on exactly what each color represents; it is up to the family to decide which colors they want. Everyone should participate in producing as beautiful a crest as they can make.

Next write up a joint "family mission statement" that describes in words what each of the symbols stands for. Finally, holding hands and looking up at the crest hanging on the wall, they each promise the group to always do their best to exhibit the traits honored there.

Variation
A few months later, the family might convene a second meeting to determine whether everyone still agrees on the symbols in the crest, or whether there is a new consensus for some other values. They may even want to make this reconsideration an annual family tradition.

ACTIVITY: Value Box

The Objective
To provide an enjoyable time for the family to engage in discussion about values.

The Situation
Maura and Tom want to teach their children the ethics and morals that they consider central to their lives. As professional teachers, they know that a conversation about the topic might be too sophisticated for their daughters, Nikki, six, and Caitlin, nine.

Materials Needed
A pack of 100 3" × 5" cards, file box to store the cards, an 8½" × 11" sheet of colored Foamcore or cardboard

so so so

The girls love to play board games, so Tom and Maura spend a few evenings devising the following game for the family. They buy a pack of 3" × 5" cards and a file box that accommodates the cards. The cards are available in a wide range of colors. Maura and the kids decorate the box as a fun introductory project. Later, Maura and Tom write down a set of hypothetical situations, one situation for each card. They design twenty situation cards as a starter pack.

Here is an example of a situation card:

You are eight years old. You are invited to a friend's house to play after school. Your parents give you permission, and arrangements are made among the adults. On the day of the play date, you and the friend walk to her house together. When you get to your friend's house, however, an adult is not home as planned, and your friend's eleven-year-old brother and two of his friends are there playing with firecrackers in the family room. You have been told not to play with matches or firecrackers, and you are frightened. The older boys want you and your friend to play with them. Your friend wants to play, too, and urges you to join in the fun. What do you do?

On a piece of Foamcore or colored cardboard, Tom and Maura list core value words, such as *courage, strength, honesty, justice, peace, love,* and others that come to mind.

Then they gather as a family and decide how much time they want to devote to the game. They set a kitchen timer to remind themselves of the time designated. They decide to begin with the youngest person, and Nikki draws a situation card from the deck. She reads the card aloud so the others all know the scenario and can think about it. She answers the question and then chooses from the list the core value word that best represents the value in question.

After Nikki is done with her turn, everyone in the family openly discusses the situation. Since this situation was something that actually happened to Tom back when he was eight, he is able to talk about his experience. Interestingly, he had chosen to play with the older boys and was punished when his friend's parents discovered the boys playing with firecrackers and called Tom's father. Tom's daughters were shocked that he had behaved in such a way, and they were delighted to have the chance to tell him the right thing to do! Tom was able to tell them how embarrassed and ashamed he had felt and how fortunate it was that he and his friends had not caused a fire or been badly hurt. He never played with firecrackers again and felt that his punishment was just.

The family continues discussing until the kitchen timer goes off.

ACTIVITY: Not-So-Trivial Pursuit

The Objective

To facilitate communication among family members and to make discussions about important family values more enticing and fun. The purpose of this game is to give everyone a chance to articulate their own view of what the family's values should be, and to hear others talk about theirs.

The Situation

Every time Sandy and Don want to discuss important topics with their fourteen-year-old twins, Amanda and Justin, the children roll their eyes, make rude remarks, or simply remain silent. Both parents feel uncomfortable talking with their children about their family's values, and unfortunately their children seem to know it. Sandy has decided to try to incorporate a discussion on family values into an imitation of their favorite family pastime: Trivial Pursuit.

Materials Needed

Trivial Pursuit game board, pieces, and dice; notebook

&~ &~ &~

First, Sandy gets the family together in a comfortable room with everyone facing West (the direction of insight and wisdom). She lights a kerosene lantern, which gives off a warm and cozy glow. She finds that a late winter afternoon in a snowstorm is the perfect time to carry out this ritual. She assigns one question to each category on the Trivial Pursuit board: blue, pink, yellow, brown, and orange. (The questions will change the next time the family plays.) Here are the questions Sandy chooses:

- Blue cards: What is something or someone our whole family can be thankful for?
- Pink cards: Who is a member of our family who has recently done something admirable?
- Yellow cards: Who is a famous person you look up to and why?
- Brown cards: What book, movie, or song can you think of that reminds you of our family?
- Orange cards: What is a fun activity that we all could do together on a Saturday?

Someone writes each of the questions into a notebook (one used specifically for this purpose), leaving plenty of space for answers. Someone else is assigned to record each person's answers in the notebook.

Everyone picks a game piece and then rolls the dice. The game proceeds as it usually does, except that the Trivial Pursuit questions are replaced by the questions assigned to the colors. Also, each person only moves once per turn, and virtually any answer that is seriously given should be considered correct. Since the questions are open-ended, it is fine that they are asked more than once, as they will be. It is not necessary to continue playing until everybody gets "home." Sandy's family quits when they feel they are ready for a discussion of the values that have been generated by this ritual.

Variation
You might want to use this game as a follow-up to the two previous activities involving the Things I Like to Do and Personal Shield forms.

ACTIVITY: A Penny Saved

The Objective
To give children the direction and experience needed to handle their financial lives and learn the value of money.

The Situation
Kenisha is a single mother of three who learned, through many years of hard work and debt repayment, the importance of understanding money management. Her parents never taught her how to responsibly handle her finances, and she is determined to teach her children what she has learned. Instead of lecturing her children about saving, Kenisha decides to design an activity that will engage her cynical fourteen-year-old, Andre, as well as her two other children, Tonya, eleven, and Shondra, eight.

Materials Needed
Forms that are designed ahead of time (see below), picnic food

¥ ¥ ¥

Conduct this ritual in August, just before the beginning of the new school year. With your children, choose a favorite outdoor place and put together a picnic of favorite foods. (Lynne's family delights in a "junk food picnic" because such foods are a rarity in our home. This is also a fairly "fuss-free" way to go!) Have each family member choose one or two favorite foods to include.

Before picnic day, make one form for each person that features lines for the year, for the person's name, and for a list of financial goals. These forms, filled out during the ritual, will be filed in a safe place once you're at home again.

On the day of the picnic, find a shady spot where you can sit in a circle and be private. Hand out the forms and explain that they are for financial planning.

Kenisha began her ritual with these words:

"We all had a great summer and next week you kids will be going back to school. Fall is traditionally a time of harvest, of gathering for the winter, of saving. This seems like a good time for us to do some planning, and I have some ideas.

"I've been giving each of you an allowance for over a year, and now I want us to work together as a family to learn about money management and saving. Andre already has a part-time job, Tonya is starting to baby sit for Mrs. Nuñez, and before we know it, Shondra will be earning an income, too. We're a family of workers, and I'm proud of us!

"I'm sorry we didn't have a real vacation together this summer, so one thing I want to do for certain is take a family trip next summer. In order to do that, we have to plan ahead as well as save up money. Can we agree on a place we'd all like to visit? How do you think we can afford to get there and have some fun?"

Kenisha leads the brainstorming that ensues and weaves a plan for saving money into her narrative. They agree to starting a coffee can "bank" the minute they get home. The children agree on their own to put a portion of their allowances into the can each week. They also list many ideas for saving money over the next year, including saving returnable bottles and cans for the deposit money. It is decided that the family will meet the following week to start planning their trip and figuring out how much it will cost so that they can begin saving toward that goal.

If your family tries Kenisha's ritual, introduce the forms ahead of time and have everyone fill in the year and his or her name. Tell them that in addition to saving for a family vacation, you would like each individual to save for something he or she wants. Have them write it down on their form. Be sure to plan a time to work with each individual on his or her personal savings goal.

Next, discuss the importance of giving to charity. Choose a charity the family would like to support, and decide how much you will give. Then decide what percentage of the total each person will give.

Some families begin a savings account for their children at birth. Others never do. During this ritual, tell your children that you will be starting (or continuing) savings accounts for each of them and that you expect them to save an amount agreed upon ahead of time, each week or month, whenever you give them their allowance. In our family, we require that our children put half their monthly allowance and earned income into savings. They are allowed to keep $10 of any gift money they receive, putting the rest into savings.

It takes parental time to help children navigate in the financial world, but the rewards are worth every minute. There are many excellent books available (see Recommended Resources) to help you with further money management activities, including investing with children.

ACTIVITY: All in a Day's Work

The Objective

To promote the value of work as a path to growing maturity and responsibility.

The Situation

One value that is of key importance to many families is a strong work ethic. It is important that both sons and daughters grow confident in their abilities to obtain and maintain a job in order to provide for themselves, as well as for their future families.

Materials Needed

Several small polished rocks, brightly designed cloth to tie up in as a bag, ribbon for tying off the bag, ripe fruit, sparkling cider

⊷⊷⊷

The evening before the first day of work for a child, the family gathers to celebrate the child's entrance into the world of work. Depending upon the family, the definition of a "first job" could be quite different —from a twelve-year-old's first newspaper route, to a teenager's supermarket job, to a college graduate's first salaried position.

Laura and Hugh's oldest child, Allison, is sixteen years old. She is a good student and has aspirations of going to a private university, although she knows that is an expensive choice. As a result, Allison has decided to get a part-time job working at the front desk of a local fitness club in order to save some money for her education as well as for other personal expenses. At ten hours per week, with additional hours over school vacations and in the summer, this job does not interfere with her studies. Allison's parents are pleased by her decision, because it seems to indicate resourcefulness and a desire for financial self-sufficiency.

On the evening before her first day at work, after their usual dinner, Laura takes out a small decorated fabric bag full of polished stones, which is tied at the top with ribbon and a silk flower. She also takes out a bottle of chilled sparkling cider, champagne glasses, and a plate of four ripe, red apples, enough for Allison, her parents, and her younger brother, and places them in the center of the table.

Hugh and Laura tell Allison how proud they are of her initiative and willingness to work. They assure her that it will put her on a path of self-reliance that will serve her well as she progresses through her schooling and professional career. Hugh gives the decorated bag with the stones to Allison, telling her that the stones symbolize the fact that work can be a burden and that it is not always fun, but that the brightly colored bag that holds them represents the strength of spirit and body that Allison will develop as a worker. The flower that ties the bag further represents the growth and promise of the future. After Allison accepts the bag, Laura hands each family member one of the apples and a glass of sparkling cider. They then toast Allison and the "fruits" of her labor.

chapter 8

Making the Ordinary Special

For most of us, special events are usually times for celebration. We often have traditional rituals for such circumstances, such as graduation ceremonies, that prescribe how we ought to behave. Turning everyday activities into special occasions is more of a challenge, however, requiring a lot of imagination. If you are successful, though, your family will feel closer, more appreciative of each other, and more joyful.

ACTIVITY: You're Special, I'm Special

The Objective
To develop a system for helping family members make each other feel loved every day.

The Situation
Too often in our busy lives, we neglect to express to our families how much we care for them. We tend to work hard creating special occasions for each other, such as birthday parties, but forget to make everyday caring for each other important. Lynne's family has a tradition that meets this need.

Materials Needed

A slip of paper for each person in the family with his or her name written on it, a bowl to hold the folded slips of paper

෴ ෴ ෴

Once a week, or at your family meeting if you have one, each person picks a name from the bowl. For the rest of the week, the person whose name is written on the slip of paper becomes a "special person" to the one who selected him or her. The purpose of this activity is to show your love for your "special person" over the course of the week in simple but meaningful ways. At the same time, you are the "special person" to the one who chose your name this week, and you will be on the receiving end of loving attention.

The first week we tried this in our family, no one could think of what to do to demonstrate caring for each other. Therefore, at our next family meeting we brainstormed a short list of the ways we might make someone feel special. We listed favorite foods we might make for each other, or favorite magazines we could get for each other. I feel special when I don't have to nag the boys to complete their daily chores, our younger son loves to have someone take the time to play a game of chess with him, our older son likes to be read to before bed, and my husband is happiest when we have peaceful family dinners without bickering.

Once we had compiled our list, it became very easy to integrate caring into our daily lives. Several times a week we check the list for our chosen special person to see how we can make his or her life a little cheerier. In this way, we all feel just a bit more loved every day.

ACTIVITY: Make Every Day a Kodak Moment

The Objective
To create memories in a fun, innovative way.

The Situation
Selena is thirteen years old, the youngest in her family; her two older sisters are Ann, sixteen, and Melissa, eighteen. Her parents were divorced when she was five, and now she and her sisters live with their mother. Because the divorce was such an emotionally painful event, she does not remember much from her childhood. In addition, there are only a few photographs of her family from earlier times. Although Selena can't do anything about the lack of photos from the past, she can do something about the future. She has persuaded her family to create their own memories in photos, starting today.

Materials Needed
A camera, or several disposable cameras (the family may want to take a trip to a wholesale store to buy disposable cameras that are cheaper in bulk); a photo album with room for people to write comments; art supplies if the family wants to decorate the photo album

⁂

At the beginning of each month, one family member is selected and given a camera to take family pictures. The photos can be candid or posed group shots—whatever the photographer believes best show the family in action. It is a chance for each family member to capture moments that aren't otherwise "special." The idea is to record ordinary moments that, when caught on film, reveal what is unique about a family.

The rules governing the kind of photos to be taken are up to the family. It is important not to disrespect anyone's privacy. What is acceptable and what is not should be decided in advance. When the film is done, it is the responsibility of the photographer to get the film developed and prints made.

Selena's mother introduced the activity this way:

"This month it's Selena's turn to take pictures of the family. As we discussed earlier, Ann is studying for her SATs every night from 7 to 9, and she would prefer that we not distract her at that time unless she tells us differently. Otherwise, Selena should use her own discretion as to what she believes makes us the Cooper family. The photos don't all have to be of us posing with smiles, they can be of us watching TV or making a messy dinner together!"

At the end of each month, the family gathers around a table to see the month's photos. The table top has been covered with a yellow cloth, chosen to symbolize the family's happiness. On top of that, two dozen or so photos are spread out. The four women discuss them with the goal of winnowing them down to the half-dozen shots they all feel are truly representative of their family's life. When the winners are chosen, the photographer gets to insert them into the album. Then comments are composed for use as labels. For example, if the family was photographed playing a board game, they may want the photo of the winner to have a caption reading, "Melissa wins another victory in the Cooper's Sunday night monopoly game!" After some months of this, the family will want to look back at earlier "issues" of their ordinary, but special, history. In time, they will get a clearer sense of who they really are.

Variation

Eventually, perhaps after a year, the family may wish to select a hand-ful of photos they believe are the best ones and make a collage to-gether. Another idea would be to make a card from one of the photos to send to their relatives and friends, accompanied by a little note written by each family member.

ACTIVITY: A Different Dinner

The Objective

To bring the family together for a really special weekly meal.

The Situation

Research indicates that in the United States today, families rarely eat dinner with each other. They may have a cooked meal, but the chil-dren are likely to eat earlier than the father, who comes home later in the evening. Also, they may eat at different times because of the tim-ing of school or athletic events. To tackle this problem, have one meal a week at which all family members eat together. Make it a special time by planning unusual menus and decor.

Materials Needed

Whatever would create a warm atmosphere, enhance conversation, and increase openness in conducting this ritual dinner: an unusual tablecloth, placemats, mood lighting. A round dinner table may be better than a square or rectangular one because it symbolizes a feeling of togetherness. Sitting on the floor or lawn sometimes may serve this purpose, too.

∽ ∽ ∽

Choose a night in the week when the whole family can assemble for dinner—maybe a Sunday night. This ritual takes a normal dinner and slowly transforms it into something special. Ideally, the ceremony should be started when the children are young and continued as they grow up. Even if ten years from now Jane will be fourteen years old and on the high school soccer team, and Steve will be seventeen and working part-time in addition to going to school, they can still plan to be home for Sunday dinner.

When this ritual is first held, the children should not be told that "from now on there is going to be a special dinner night." Instead, Jane and Steve can gradually become aware of the change by, for example, being encouraged to help cook the meal. Slowly it should dawn on them that something extraordinary is beginning to take shape. As long as something is done to make the meal unusual, that will suffice. You might decide to have one family member (or more) be in charge of dinner and another be in charge of dessert, with an alternating list each week.

Before the meal begins, family members might take turns finding a prayer and bringing it to the meal. If possible, the meal should take place in a different room from the one in which the family normally eats. Create a soothing atmosphere by lowering the lighting and playing soft music in the background. Since most families are so used to having a fast-paced life during the week, a truly calm environment can enhance the realization that this meal is unique. Go out of your way to cook or bake a special food.

Different things can be done to close the meal, after the family has cleared the table together. To create a sense of belonging, each family member might end by stating an intention or a goal for that week, or by naming something positive that they hope to do for another family member. One of the children might lead the family in a song. Another might take everyone on a walk to the park after the meal and give them a view of the stars through a telescope.

ACTIVITY: Lynne's Family Fun Day

The Objective
To enjoy the company of each other doing activities we love.

The Situation
It seems as though we used to spend a lot more time together as a family before our boys were teenagers. As they grew more independent and their interests developed, they began doing things with other families and spending more time with their friends. Before we knew it, we seldom saw our children together in the same place at the same time! As a remedy, we invented the following tradition.

Materials Needed
Dependent upon the activity chosen

❧❧❧

We commit to spending one day together doing something exciting each month. At one of our weekly family meetings, we randomly assign a month to each person, and it is that person's responsibility to find a fun activity for all of us to do sometime during his or her month. Since there are four of us, each of us is responsible for three months a year.

We can choose to do as a family anything affordable that sounds enjoyable. So far, no one has wanted to do something unsafe. We have tried some new things and have enjoyed going to a driving range, batting cages, movies, and the circus. We've also biked a strenuous trail and visited a restored colonial village for a day. Other activities might include baking, starting a board game family tournament, building a snowman, cooking a gourmet dinner, or acting out a play.

Some of the ideas presented by individuals in our family have been greeted by unwelcome groans, but when we actually begin trying something different, we learn a lot about each other and about the definition of fun!

ACTIVITY: Bedtime

The Objective
To design a bedtime ritual that is calming and brings a gentle end to the day.

The Situation
Bedtime can be fraught with tension, frazzled nerves, and overtired little ones as well as parents. It is tempting to rush through the bedtime routine so that you can collapse on the couch for a little respite before sinking into bed yourself.

Materials Needed
Storybook, lavender-scented candle, audiotape of lullabies

∾ ∾ ∾

When it is time for your child to go to sleep, ideally after a warm bath, curl up in his or her bed for a short story. Don't choose anything scary or something that may need a lot of explanation. After the story, turn out the lights in the room, light the lavender-scented candle and share a moment of silence while holding hands. With the candle still lit, ask your child the following questions: "What was one nice thing someone did for you today?" "What was one nice thing you did for someone else today?" "What is one thing you are grateful for today?" After asking the questions, blow out the candle and either sing to your child or play a tape of lullabies as he or she drifts off to sleep (and perhaps you, too!).

We have been doing some version of this ritual with our children since they were born, and have never had bedtime struggles with either of them. Now our children are ten and fifteen years old. We still do an adaptation of this ritual with them. It has become as meaningful to us as it is to them.

chapter 9

Practicing Pragmatic Skills

Many of the life skills we want and need to teach our children are some of life's more tedious chores. As adults we approach them as such, and our children, in turn, perceive them the same way. By creating new traditions, whether daily, weekly, or seasonally, the mundane can be transformed into a rich experience for the whole family.

ACTIVITY: Day Planner

The Objective
To help a child develop planning skills that will have lifelong benefits.

The Situation
Children who are organized and plan their time well are better students. They are also more likely to cope well with the rigors of balancing school and extracurricular activities such as sports.

Brianna is eight years old. Her parents, Richard and Simone, want to increase her awareness of the scheduling that is necessary in their family to accomplish all that they want and need to do. Their hope is that Brianna will gradually learn to manage her own time. Right now, she shows little awareness of how long it takes to finish her homework, how much time it takes to eat a meal, or the amount of time needed to drive to a friend's house for a play date. Brianna is often frustrated from trying to squeeze too much into her young life.

Materials Needed

A pre-made calendar with large spaces for writing daily memos, or the materials or software to create your own calendar if you choose

੪ ੪ ੪

Richard purchased inexpensive calendar-making software, a package of stickers, and a set of markers at an office supply store. He made a large wall calendar for Brianna, with each day a 3-inch-square box.

On New Year's Day, after a delicious brunch, Simone and Richard sat down with Brianna and her favorite dessert and presented the calendar to her. Richard explained that they wanted to help Brianna plan her time, and that they would be meeting as a family each Sunday evening to plan the upcoming week. He showed Brianna his electronic calendar, and Simone explained her daily planner, too. Brianna was thrilled with the gift and began decorating the January page right away.

The next Sunday evening, they gathered around the kitchen table with their calendars and talked about their plans. Simone noticed there were already complications with some of Brianna's plans.

"Brianna, if you want to have a play date with Grace on Saturday, that's okay, but we should invite her to our house instead of you going to her house since you have hockey practice in the morning and she lives a half-hour away." It was easy for Brianna to see that she didn't have enough time for extended play with her friend in another town unless a change was made. Simone's suggestion worked perfectly, and Brianna said she would play at Grace's another time. Brianna wrote those plans on her calendar and used a hockey puck sticker on each day she had hockey practice. Similarly, a piano sticker went onto the days when she had a piano lesson. Twenty minutes later, the week was planned. The whole family understood the week ahead and felt relaxed, even though it was a busy week.

Every morning at breakfast, the family took a minute to review the day with Brianna. Simone always began by saying, for example, "Today is Thursday, April 5, and it's going to be a great day!" She felt that reinforced for Brianna what day it was, and therefore what the plan was for that day.

Richard and Simone also instituted several other time management techniques including what they call "the 24-hour rule." They requested that Brianna please ask them 24 hours in advance of wanting a ride somewhere. She had gotten into the habit of making plans with friends in school and wanting a ride to a friend's house the minute she got home. Brianna was then often disappointed to learn that her parents were unable to accommodate her. They also decided that each day Brianna had homework (Monday through Thursday) would be a TV-free day, and that her homework had to be done right after school.

By making several family policies and planning their time together, Brianna soon learned that she really did have plenty of time to do the things she wanted to do, and she also had time to complete her schoolwork and outside activities. These are important habits that will follow Brianna through secondary schooling and into the complicated work world someday. Simone and Richard even found their family planning time helped the two of them organize their lives better.

ACTIVITY: May I Take Your Order?

The Objective

To teach children basic finances and manners required for adult competence and give them a sense of accomplishment.

The Situation

Molly, Nick, and Sam, ages eight, ten, and twelve respectively, are good helpers around the house. They pick up after themselves, help out with cleanup after dinner, and make their beds every morning. Their parents, Chuck and Rita, want to expand the children's practical skills beyond routine chores. They want to include more complicated "grown-up" tasks. They feel that exposing the kids to everyday situations involving finances and social customs is necessary for raising competent, independent adults. Chuck and Rita are looking for an enjoyable way to incorporate some important practical skills into the children's play. They came up with the idea of opening "Chez Molly, Nick & Sam," a pretend restaurant that the kids will run for one afternoon, with minimal help from adults.

Materials Needed

Groceries for a lunch, computer (optional)

෬ ෬ ෬

First, Chuck and Rita call Molly, Nick, and Sam together in the kitchen on Saturday morning and introduce the idea: "We think it's time you kids learned something about money, but at the same time, we want you to have fun. For this afternoon only, we want you to open a restaurant here in our house and serve lunch for us and Aunt Sue and Uncle Bob. You get to decide what's on the menu. We'll give you a certain amount of money and you'll have to figure out what ingredients you can afford to buy with that amount. We'll go with you to buy the food. Then you'll have to decide how much to charge for everything. You'll want to choose enough to make back the money you spend on the ingredients and also make a little profit. Would you like to do that?"

The children respond enthusiastically to the idea. They confer with each other to create a menu. Chuck and Rita go with them to the grocery store to buy the food needed. Then, several conversations about the best way to spend the money ensue.

After they purchase the groceries the needs, they decide on the cost of each menu item:

- *Entrees: Peanut butter and jelly sandwiches ($1) or cold meat sandwiches ($1.35).*

- *Dessert: Cookies and chocolate ice cream with sprinkles ($.90) or cupcakes filled with whipped cream ($.85)*

- *Beverages: Iced tea, milk, or club soda ($.35 each).*

Sam knows how to use the computer with a graphics program, so with his help they design and print out several copies of the menu (old-fashioned paper and felt tip markers also work). The kids dole out tasks: Nick and Sam set the table, fold the napkins, and tidy up the room where the "restaurant" will be. Molly assists them with the proper placement of utensils.

At noon, Chuck, Rita, Aunt Sue, and Uncle Bob arrive at Chez Molly, Nick & Sam. Molly dressed up for the occasion. She welcomes them, takes them to their table, and gives them their menus. Molly takes their orders, goes to the kitchen, and helps Sam and Nick prepare the orders. She attends to their requests ("Aunt Sue needs a clean fork—it dropped on the floor!," and "Chuck would like a second cup of iced tea with his dessert").

When the meal is completed, Nick and Sam make out a bill and Molly presents it to the diners. Rita asks to speak to the chefs and congratulates them and Molly on their excellent service and cuisine.

Finally, the adults talk with the children, asking them what they have learned and how they might do it differently another time.

ACTIVITY: Calm Down!

The Objective
To help each other learn some effective calming techniques.

The Situation
In our fast-paced society, it is often hard to think straight. When we are overly stressed, it can affect our work, family, and health. Learning relaxation and calming techniques can prove beneficial in many stressful situations.

The Gonzales family lives in a suburb of Los Angeles. The father, Jose, has to travel many days a week and is not happy with his current job. Sara, the mother, works part-time to help provide for their three children. Danita, who is sixteen, often worries about people not liking her. Her younger brother Roberto, who is fourteen, has a problem dealing with anger. Eleven-year-old James has been getting into a lot of trouble at school and is experiencing excessive anxiety. No member of the family has much time even to share their thoughts with the others, much less have fun together. After some careful thinking, Jose and Sara decide that what the family really needs is to learn some ways they can help each other calm down.

Materials Needed
Index cards and pen or pencil for each participant, assorted magazines, large sheet of paper

ᔫ ᔫ ᔫ

The family gathers in the living room, and Sara says,

"I think we're all agreed that our lives are too stressful and we need to find some ways to calm down. I have done some reading, and I have discovered two activities that I think will help each of us to handle better the tensions that we face almost every day. I would like it if each of you would try these two exercises, and then we can talk about whether they're helpful or not. This is not just for the kids; Papa, you try it, too.

"First, close your eyes and imagine as many as seven peaceful scenes. Next, write a phrase describing each scene on a different index card. If you need help imagining a scene, you might want to choose some of the scenes from these magazines:"

1. Waves on the shore
2. A field of wheat blowing in the land
3. Glowing embers in a fireplace
4. The view from a high hill
5. A brook babbling down the side of a mountain in spring
6. A flower garden
7. The park over on Washington Street

Instruct everyone to arrange the cards from most to least tranquil. "Now let's each read what phrase you wrote for your number 1 peaceful scene, and also have you describe it in some detail. I'm going to write down what each person says on this large piece of paper."

They go through each person's list of scenes until they have all been described. Sara suggests that they each memorize their own list (they can add or substitute a scene from someone else's wish if they like) and practice visualizing each scene. Later, when they feel anxious, they can visualize each place on the list sequentially, and each step will help them to calm down.

"Now," Sara says, "I'm going to tell you about another kind of relaxation exercise. Of course, relieving our tensions by harming others is unacceptable. However, punishing something that represents the upsetting situation can be healthy. I would like each of you to draw a picture of a stressful situation or person. In other words, draw a picture of something or someone that makes you scared or angry."

When everyone is finished, Sara tells them to pin their drawings to one of the old couch cushions or pillows that she has provided. She asks them to punch their drawing as much as they feel is necessary to relieve their feelings of stress.

"Okay," said Sara, "what to you think of these two techniques for calming your nerves?" Everyone agrees that the relaxation methods felt like they might work. For the rest of this session, Sara and her family practice composing some new mental pictures of peaceful scenes and using them to calm down.

Variation
People can try putting their drawings on the floor and stamping on them, crushing them into a ball, or scribbling on them.

ACTIVITY: John's Thunderstorm Medal

The Objective
To alleviate a child's specific fear, such as a phobia.

The Situation
A "Thunderstorm Medal" helps a child to handle a specific fearful situation such as a fear of thunderstorms. It imbues a medal or other

amulet with the power to calm anxious feelings (see chapter 3). It worked wonderfully when my granddaughter had this problem.

Materials Needed

An object that can be held in the hand, such as a medal or foreign coin; a tape recording of thunder; one candle for each participant

          🙶 🙶 🙶

Organize a meeting of your whole family, explaining to them in advance that you will be imbuing an object with the power to alleviate your child's fear. Ask them to consider what they might want to say as advice and best wishes for your child's serenity. Their hopes will empower the amulet to be effective. They will have a chance to share their ideas during the ceremony.

Convene the family around your family's altar or a low table covered in a blue cloth to suggest tranquility. In the center, place the fanciest plate you own. Put the amulet you have chosen in the center of the plate. Surround the plate with unlit candles, one for each person who is participating. Darken the room. Reading with a flashlight, introduce the ritual in the following way:

"We are gathered here today because we want to help Anna. We all want to help her not to be so afraid of the noisy thunder. The way we are going to help her is by putting magic into the special medal that is in the center of this plate. We're going to bless it, and we are going to put our strongest wishes into it so that it can protect her from being frightened. Grammy, would you be the first one to say what wish you want to put into Anna's medal?"

In a kindly and gentle voice, the participants in this ceremony take turns stating their ideas of how the child can learn to calm her fears when she hears thunder. They state their hopes and wishes that she will be able to overcome her anxiety. If they like, they may promise to say a prayer for her. While talking, they place the fingertips of their right hand on the amulet. As family members finish making their statements, they light one of the candles.

"Now, Anna, to make sure that the magic wishes stay in the medal, you must blow out all the candles."

When she has finished blowing out the candles, tell her to take the medal and hold it in the palm of in her hand. Tell her that if she really believes in it, the medal will protect her from being afraid. Then inform her that you're going to play the sound of thunder on the tape recorder.

"Anna, when you start to hear this sound of the thunder, take the medal into your hand, and remember what everyone has said here today. We are all right there with you, taking care of you, helping you to feel safe. When you do this, we want you to breathe slowly and try to relax the muscles in your body. The medal will help you to do that. When you hear the thunder, try your best to relax. Let's try it now."

Turn on a tape recording of thunder. If you can't find one, shaking a baking sheet may work. As the tape is played, rest your fingers lightly on your child's wrist. When the thunder begins to play, you will probably notice an increase in her pulse. As she thinks about the medal and slows her breathing, her pulse rate should decline. It may not return to normal—that will take some practice. When she has practiced this with some success, tell her to keep the medal by her bed and use it to help keep the thunder from frightening her anymore.

For about a year, my granddaughter kept her medal beside her bed and held it whenever she heard the rumble of thunder. Now she no longer needs it, and it resides in her "special stuff" box.

Variation

If the child's fears do not abate substantially, you should reconvene the original group and let the child explain how she is feeling about thunderstorms, or whatever it is that is making her anxious. Then you redo the ritual as before, telling her to try as hard she can to believe in the power of the amulet and to feel the support of those who love her.

ACTIVITY: Family Homework Time

The Objective

To ease the end-of-day tensions and make evening time more pleasurable and productive for the family.

The Situation

Marion is the mother of two young children, Brendan, four and a half, and Casey, seven. Although not a single parent, Marion feels like one, because her husband, Dave, works the 3 to 11 P.M. shift and commutes seventeen miles to his job in the suburbs. This schedule worked well for them when the children were younger, but now that Casey is in school and beginning to get more complicated homework, Marion feels pressured to help him with his homework while trying simultaneously to manage Brendan's bedtime routine. She also finds that her time to do the family's paperwork (bill paying, letter writing, planning) has been squeezed out almost entirely.

Materials Needed

A round table or dining room table, supplies for completing homework (keep in a basket close to the table: pens, pencils, a pencil sharpener, erasers, a ruler, a stapler, scissors, glue sticks, anything else that you and your child may need close by), a snack that everyone likes, each individual's homework or paperwork

& & &

Marion and Dave decide to sit down one night and work out a schedule for Marion to try on school nights. They come up with a plan that Marion tries for a week.

First, dinner is eaten an hour earlier, so that the children's bedtime doesn't get too late. The children are hungry by 5 P.M. anyway, so Marion decides that instead of a snack at that time, she will prepare something simple for the three of them to eat. After dinner, she has the boys help her with cleaning the kitchen. Brendan can clear the table, Marion will rinse the dishes and load the dishwasher, and Casey will put away leftovers. Next is what they now call "family homework time."

Casey gets his homework out and Marion helps him get started with the simpler tasks. Then she helps Brendan with his "homework." Brendan likes to draw and do other kinds of artwork. Marion has packed a small backpack with art supplies and some inexpensive preschool-level workbooks that help preschoolers learn their numbers and letters. On this night Marion gives Brendan a workbook page to do and a sticker book to decorate. Then she puts out a plate of cookies and makes a favorite milkshake for each of them.

(A quick and delicious "milkshake" that our family loves is the Indian drink, lassi or lassa. Mix flavored yogurt such as vanilla, lemon, or maple with a flavored seltzer water such as lemon, lime, or orange. Play with the proportions until the drink is as thick as a milkshake.)

After settling the children, Marion goes to her homework basket, where she keeps unpaid bills and other family business such as letter writing. Since Marion is sitting at the table with the boys, she is available to answer questions and mediate any squabbles that arise between the two. After a half-hour, Marion helps the boys pack their backpacks and assists Casey with choosing a book for his fifteen minutes of silent reading time (recommended by his teacher). While Casey reads quietly on the couch, Marion gets Brendan ready for bed.

At bedtime, Casey, who is very proud of his reading ability, reads the family a story. Marion turns out the lights in the living room at the end of the story and asks for a moment of silence while she lights a candle. The family then says together these simple words, "Thank you, God, for giving us strong minds and loving hearts. Tonight we worked together to help us grow stronger as a family." Then Marion puts Brendan to bed and has time to read a chapter of the book she and Casey have started together.

When Dave and Marion have an opportunity to discuss the new system, Marion reports that she is amazed by how much work she has accomplished in that first week. Casey is getting his work done without resistance and Brendan is delighted to be part of the effort. Marion is certain that Brendan is not only learning a lot but is also developing an important habit that will help prepare him for school when he begins in the fall. She is very enthusiastic about the future of family homework time!

ACTIVITY: Seasonal Organization Blitz

The Objective
To teach children (and parents) valuable organization skills.

The Situation
Rob and Suzanne are the parents of very active four-year-old twin boys, Troy and Bryan, and their six-year-old sister, Haley. Things quickly get out of hand in their busy household, with toys scattered throughout the house in piles several layers deep. The whole

family feels completely overwhelmed and frustrated by the mess. The children can't find coveted toys when they want them, and the parents can't find important papers when they need them.

Materials Needed

Containers as necessary for organization, favorite foods for the feast

~ ~ ~

Suzanne and Rob realize that they are fairly typical of the middle-class American family in that they have a lot of "stuff." With three children close in age and not much time to think about alternatives, the family has acquired many more toys than their children can play with at one time, a lot of them gifts from well-meaning extended family and friends. Rob and Suzanne decide to design what they call a "seasonal organizational blitz" to manage their possessions, and thus take control of their lives.

Before they began working with their children, they needed to spend several evenings together figuring out an organizational system for the family. They used a book for guidance (see Recommended Resources) and discovered that it was important that each of the children's possessions have a home that the young children could access on their own.

Once the possessions had been assigned homes, they bought containers for the things that could be containerized, especially the small toys such as Duplos, Tinkertoys, and blocks. Then they labeled the containers with pictures as well as words, since only Haley knew how to read.

Early in the spring, they were ready to have their first seasonal gathering: a celebratory feast with foods they all loved. They followed the meal with dessert and a discussion of what toys could be put away in storage (in their case, the attic) for the season. With some toys this was easy. The children clearly saw that sleds and skis could be put away in the spring, being replaced by bikes and rollerblades. It was harder for them to put away or get rid of some of their other toys. Troy, in particular, wanted to hang on to everything he had ever acquired. Rob had an idea that helped. He told the kids that he would help them organize a toy sale that they will hold on their front porch later in the spring. The kids would be able to split the profits and each buy a new small toy with the money they earned. This made them all happy. Next, the family walked through each room and decided what toys, puzzles, and games they wanted to put in the sale. They also decided which playthings could be put in the attic until the next season. That way, if there was a toy that someone really wanted to play with, it would not be difficult to retrieve.

Rob and Suzanne realized that there is more to keeping organized than revolving their possessions from storage back into the active household, then back to storage. They also need to manage better what was coming into the home.

They talked to the kids about how fortunate their family is to have so many wonderful things and that there were many, many children who have almost nothing. They told the children that for their birthdays, Rob and Suzanne would like to celebrate their family's plentitude by having the party guests give to children who don't have very many toys. So Haley, Bryan, and Troy would still have a traditional party with their friends, but instead of getting gifts, the gifts brought by their guests would go to an orphanage. Suzanne explained that the guests will be told on the invitation that the gifts are for children in an orphanage. Rob told them that the family would also celebrate birthdays with the birthday child, and that this would be the time when the child receives gifts for him- or herself. Suzanne hoped that this new way of celebrating birthdays would help her children build a sense of giving to those who have little.

Rob instituted a new pick-up rule in addition to the organization blitz. The children are now taught to pick up their toys from one adventure before moving on to the next activity. The family also decided that every day before dinner, they will spend ten minutes picking up as a family.

Suzanne said that they had done such a great job with their first blitz that they would celebrate with a Saturday trip to the local children's museum. She explained that they would have blitzes every season starting with a feast and ending with a family outing. She congratulated the kids for their hard work and told them that they had made some really tough decisions about their toys. Rob expressed how thoughtful he felt they each were for celebrating their birthdays with those less fortunate than they were and by donating some of their baby toys to younger cousins. Bryan, Haley, and Troy felt very grown up to have participated in the difficult decision making.

chapter 10

Improving School-Related Situations

There was a time when the typical student's greatest fear was getting caught chewing gum in class and being ordered to stick it to her or his nose. Now many kids worry about their personal safety at school. The growing tensions common at all grade levels interfere with the concentration and sense of well-being of our children.

Of course, there are many other situations at school besides safety issues that parents can help with. Some of them are unpleasant—difficulties with teachers, clannishness of peer groups, and learning problems. Other events are cause for celebration—making new friends, acing a test, and winning the city championship. Here we try to assist you by describing rituals that alleviate some of the hurts that are caused by being in school.

ACTIVITY: No! I Don't Want to Go!

The Objective
To creatively help young children overcome the "first day of school" jitters.

The Situation
LaShayna and Terrence have two children. Their four-year-old, Willie, is starting preschool next month. He will go to school for three or four hours, three days a week. LaShayna has been talking with him about all the new friends he will make and the things he will learn. Since LaShayna has been mentioning school to Willie, he has become more attached to her. He clings to her when they are out, and when she is not within earshot at home he becomes anxious. LaShayna is not sure what to do. School is only a month away, and her son is much more fearful of it than she had expected.

Materials Needed
None

⁂

Willie plays well with other children, and he has not exhibited anxious behavior when left with babysitters. LaShayna and Terrence are not sure why he is so nervous about school. LaShayna decides to experiment.

She visits with her neighbor, Paula, who has a son about Willie's age. They talk for a short time and LaShayna asks Paula if she can watch Willie for a couple of hours. She tells Willie good-bye and leaves. When she returns two hours later, Willie is his usual self, with no sense of fear or anxiety. Paula reports that Willie and her son had a great time playing, as they always do. Everything went smoothly. LaShayna tries this with other relatives and friends. Willie is fine in all instances.

She then takes him to a play group at the local library. When she says good-bye and turns to leave, she feels Willie clinging to her leg. This is a new play group for him. There is one other child there that he recognizes from his neighborhood. It is clear to LaShayna that Willie, like many of us, is nervous about unfamiliar surroundings and new people. LaShayna stays for a while to help him get acclimated.

Once he seems engaged, she slips out and returns an hour later. Willie is very talkative about his new group and what they learned about dinosaurs. LaShayna uses this opportunity to tell him that school is going to be a lot like that. Of course, he is not immediately convinced.

Over the next few weeks, LaShayna organizes several sessions with Willie to address his fears. They begin their time together by playing a favorite card game. During this focused time, Willie is able to relate and express some of his fears.

Next, she walks the route they will be taking to school so that he can become familiar with it. They say hello to neighbors, and LaShayna is able to point out some "landmarks" to Willie, such as Mr. Walker's red front door, the blinking yellow light, the corner store, and other neighborhood favorites.

LaShayna also takes him to his new preschool on an afternoon when the children have already gone home, so that he can visit with his new teacher, play in the block area, and draw a picture for his teacher. His teacher shows him the hook where he will hang his jacket and the "cubby" with his name above it. She gives him a dinosaur sticker to place next to his name card, so that everyone will know one of his interests. She also tells him that a lot of the children like to bring a favorite stuffed animal from home. She mentions that the stuffie (as she called it) can stay with him until circle time, then it will keep his cubby warm until it is time to go home. Next, the teacher takes Willie outside to the play yard, where he plays on the climbing structure while LaShayna talks to her about her concerns.

The next day, LaShayna and Terrence make a list with Willie of all the things he is looking forward to doing at school. He is enthusiastic about many of the things he saw on his visit. Terrence and two-year-old Tiara, Willie's sister, are able to join LaShayna and Willie on some of their walks to school, where Willie and Tiara play on the playground several more times before the first day of school.

On one trip, they meet another new student at the playground. LaShayna invites the little girl for a play date the next day so that Willie will have at least one friend at school. Nicole, the new friend, and Willie have a great time planning which stuffies they want to accompany them on their first day.

LaShayna promises Willie that every day after school, they will have special time together while Tiara naps. They will talk about his school day and do a fun activity together before his dad comes home and she has to leave for work. Now Willie looks forward to his school day and to special time with his mom in the afternoon.

ACTIVITY: Report Card Party

The Objective
To develop a positive attitude toward school report cards.

The Situation
Can you remember bringing home a report card? How did you feel just before you received your card from your teacher? For many students, report cards cause trepidation and unpleasant recriminations. Even those of us who did well in school can probably remember wor-

rying about what grades we were going to get, and can recall our parents saying, "This is good but we know you can do better."

How would it be if, instead, the end of a report period were viewed as a time of celebration? After all, the child receiving the report card has just spent several months trying to learn the things that we adults consider important. Instead of intimidation, wouldn't it be better if we were to express our appreciation and encouragement to the child for doing the work, even if the outcome wasn't particularly successful? Most children do respond better to a pat on the back than to criticism.

Materials Needed
Lunch, a small table, bubbles and wand

ભ ભ ભ

On a Saturday after your children have brought home their report cards, bring the family together for a special lunch. Place a small table near the dining table in the southeast corner of the dining room. East represents the planting of new seeds, and South is emblematic of growth. You are also combining the basic elements of air and fire, which are associated with East and South. Represent fire by serving some spicy dish as the main luncheon entree. For air, you could startle your family by coming into the room blowing bubbles from a child's bubble-making wand. This will get their attention, and signify that something new and different is about to take place. You might want to explain this symbolism to your family, or just leave it as a subtle undertone to suggest that you want to encourage a new attitude toward bringing home report cards as well as fostering your children's educational growth.

Put your children's report cards in the center of the table. Before lunch starts, make the following statement:

"Your mother [father] and I want to say how much we appreciate the efforts you kids have put into your schoolwork. In our family, we believe that learning what you need to know to be a successful person and good citizen in our community is very important. We can see from your report cards that each of you has had some worthwhile achievements, but also have some areas where you may need some help [Adapt this sentence to be accurate, but also positive]. Let's talk about each of your report cards and brainstorm about what help our family can give each of you so you can continue to improve."

Now read a prepared statement, summarizing what was noteworthy about each of your children's report cards. It is a good idea to advise your youngest child first, because after an older child has given some advice to a younger sister or brother, she or he is more likely to accept advice when her or his turn comes. Make statements like, "We are so proud of Bernice's improved grades in history and math. It looks like she could use some advice about how to do better in science. Bernice, what is your biggest problem with science?" After she has spoken, ask, "Does anyone have any ideas about things she might try so she can understand science better?"

Remembering that you're celebrating the effort of the schoolwork, do your best to remain positive. After each child's report card has been discussed by the family, serve the special lunch, following up with cake and ice cream.

You probably have one child who consistently makes higher grades than your other children. It is quite common for children within the same family to have different strengths. Make it a point to reinforce any evidence of effort as well as good grades.

Variation

You might want to make this exercise a tradition at the end of each report period. Use your imagination to make each celebration of your children's schoolwork fresh and enticing.

ACTIVITY: My Teacher Hates Me!

The Objective

To help a child who is having problems with his or her teacher.

The Situation

Jared is a nine-year-old boy who is in the fourth grade at his large suburban elementary school. An average student, he has never complained about school before and seems to have enjoyed fourth grade up until this point, midway through the school year. He is socially adept, with many friends—both boys and girls. For several weeks, Jared has not wanted to go to school because he says his teacher hates him.

Materials Needed

None

       ∿ ∿ ∿

Jared's dad, Tony, is a single father with two other children, Ian, three, and Melissa, eleven. After the death of his wife two years ago, Tony and his children constructed a small altar where they could pray and light candles in their mother's memory. With the help of a grief counselor, Tony also began a weekly spiritual time with the children; they were not affiliated with any organized religion.

 When Jared first began complaining of difficulty with his teacher, Tony listened with only one ear. He had occasionally heard complaints about school before, and considered them a part of being a student. Tony liked Jared's teacher and remembered how fond of Mr. Thomson Melissa had been two years before. In fact, Tony felt Melissa had shouldered her grief over her mother's death better in part because of Mr. Thomson's sensitivity.

But then Jared began experiencing stomachaches and sore throats and missing school regularly. He was falling behind in his schoolwork, and the family's au pair reported that by 10 o'clock in the morning Jared seemed fine. Tony made an appointment to talk with Mr. Thomson.

Mr. Thomson showed concern over Jared's recent absences and was surprised to learn that Jared believed he didn't like him. The teacher felt that more work was expected of students in the fourth grade than in previous years, and that Jared was struggling with that expectation. He said that he had to be strict with his class of twenty-seven children and that he did occasionally single out Jared, who liked to talk with his friends more than attend to his work in class. Mr. Thomson admitted that he was having some difficulty with Jared, but that he was doing his best and that when Jared was engaged in his learning, he was bright and a pleasure to have in class. The two men brainstormed to come up with ways they could support Jared's efforts and help him realize that Mr. Thomson did like him.

That night, Tony discussed the meeting with Jared. Jared was happy to hear that Mr. Thomson did indeed like him, but he still felt that he was singled out as "the bad guy" for every small offense he committed. Tony explained that maintaining control in a classroom with twenty-seven children was a huge job, and that Mr. Thomson wanted Jared's help. Jared was interested.

Mr. Thomson had suggested that Jared be a classroom helper in several ways. First, he wanted Jared to take the completed attendance sheet to the main office every morning, which meant he had to be in school every morning. Next, he wanted Jared to write the homework assignments on the chalkboard before morning recess, so that the class could copy down the assignment when they came back inside. He also hoped that Jared would serve as a tutor in his math group since math was his strongest subject. Mr. Thomson hoped that Jared could answer some of the group's questions and write down the ones he couldn't answer for Mr. Thomson's attention later.

Tony watched Jared's face carefully as he told him the new ideas. Jared was clearly thrilled with the plan. Tony also gave Jared a small polished stone that he had blessed with his love and his wishes for Jared to feel better about school. Jared was to carry the stone in his pocket and hold it whenever he felt he wasn't doing well in school. It would remind him of his father's caring. Tony said they would follow up on the plan at their next family meeting and would continue to make a "school check-in" a regular part of the meeting for Jared, and for Melissa, too.

ACTIVITY: School's Out for Summer!

The Objective
To preserve the schoolwork of children in a creative, organized way that will show their progress throughout their school years.

The Situation
Every school day kids bring home backpacks full of papers. Before you know it, the refrigerator is covered with pictures, and every horizontal surface has a pile of homework assignments and reports. Some may be the barely recognizable efforts of a preschool child, and some may represent the extensive productions of a high school teen.

Materials Needed

A picnic, an artist's portfolio or a large plastic container with a lid, a waterproof marker, an old bureau with several drawers

❧ ❧ ❧

When your child arrives home from school each day, ask her to empty her backpack. Together, sort through the papers, keeping any that she is proud of or that you especially like. Mark the date, the child's name, and a brief description on the kept paperwork for future reference. This is especially important if you have more than one child. You may think at the time that Timmy's castle drawings are unique, but in five years, his castles may look very much like younger brother Patrick's! Recycle the unwanted papers and then, in true American fashion, display the really special pieces on the refrigerator with magnets. Anything that doesn't go on the refrigerator, place in the drawer of a bureau that is used only for this purpose. Each child should have his or her own labeled drawer.

If your child brings home three-dimensional projects such as birdhouses or terrariums, take a snapshot of the project with the proud artist and start a small photo album that is just for this purpose. Keep the project as long as it still feels special (or is still alive!), knowing that there is a record of it in your child's album.

When school is over in May or June, have a family picnic in the backyard or on the living room floor. Bring out each child's drawer from the bureau, and review together the work of the past school year. Over the course of the year, you have probably accumulated a full drawer for each child. Now is the time to be more selective about what to save in permanent storage. You may discover that your child drew dozens of pictures of butterflies or superheroes. Choose a representative sample from these multiple drawings to keep forever. Be sure the child's name and the date are on each drawing. Look at school papers from the beginning of the year and compare them to work done in June. The amount of growth that took place through the academic year will be quite obvious to you and your child.

After each child has had a chance to go through his or her drawer, place the year's work in a portfolio labeled with the child's name. Portfolios, available from art supply stores, are very large envelopes made from either paperboard or plastic and used for protecting artwork. Typically, they have handles for carrying and a flap like an envelope that closes with ties. The portfolio can be stored in a child's bedroom or in any dry storage area.

Instead of a portfolio, you may want to use a large translucent plastic container, such as those designed for sweater storage. These containers keep valuable papers dry and are less likely to get damaged than portfolios. They can be stacked in a storage area, and, since they are translucent, you can easily see what's inside. Write the artist's name in indelible marker on the outside of the container.

Use the picnic to celebrate the end of schoolwork. Mark the occasion with words such as, "Each of you learned so much in school this past year. It's clear to us that you put a lot of effort into your work and are proud of what you learned. We're proud of you, too, and now you're ready to move into the next grade. Let's celebrate!" Be sure to mention at least one skill each child worked on during the year. One child may have mastered algebra while another learned cursive writing. At the end-of-school picnic, give each child in your family the gift of a book to begin their summer reading program.

ACTIVITY: Staying on Track

The Objective

To help children appreciate differences among people in a nonjudgmental way, without either making fun of others or seeing them as "superior" or "inferior." (This activity is probably best done with children in late childhood or early adolescence, depending on their maturity level.)

The Situation

Mario is twelve years old and has just entered sixth grade. He has always done well in school, particularly in math and English, and he prides himself on being a good student. Mario and his fellow students took a math placement exam at the beginning of the year to determine in which of three math sections they belong—Advanced, Regular, or Remedial—and today in homeroom, each student received a card with his or her math section noted. The terms *Advanced, Regular,* and *Remedial* are replaced with euphemistic names: Lions, Cheetahs, and Tigers, respectively. Most of his friends are in the Cheetahs section, although a few of them are Tigers. Mario finds out that he is in the Lions section with very few other students, most of whom he has always considered "nerdy."

While Mario's parents, Denzel and Juanita, were initially thrilled about their son's success, lately they have noticed him saying things like, "I never knew how dumb all my friends were!" or "Well, I guess I have more time to go out and have fun since school comes so much easier to me!" His brother Miguel (age ten), also a superior student, is beginning to imitate him. His parents feel that his math placement is causing him to label his friends, and so they decide to expose him to an experience that might make him more open-minded.

Materials Needed

None

❧❧❧

One Saturday afternoon, Denzel and Juanita tell Mario and Miguel that they have a surprise for them. The family drives into the city to a community center, where there are several classrooms of students of various ages who are trying to learn English as their second language. Denzel and Juanita have arranged for their family to help as volunteers today. While his parents work with the adults, helping them write cover letters for job interviews, Mario is given the task of reading two large, colorful books to five- and six-year-olds; Miguel looks on.

At first, both boys are upset with their parents for making them go, as they would rather be watching sports on TV. The young children pay close attention to the reading and try hard to comprehend what they are hearing. After the reading is finished, the children descend upon Mario and Miguel to ask them questions about their lives. Some of the kids are difficult to understand, but the boys do their best. Although they do not admit it initially to their parents, Mario and Miguel really begin to enjoy themselves.

Eventually the family leaves and goes to one of the boys' favorite restaurants for lunch. They discuss the different things that each of them learned about the people with whom they worked that day. Denzel and Juanita point out how hard it is for one of the parents they helped to find employment in the United States. Even though the man has an advanced degree in his country of origin, he can't get a job because he is just beginning to learn English.

They ask the boys whether or not the children had seemed stupid to them since they were having such a hard time with English. Mario admits that at first he did think so, but he came to see that his judgment was wrong. Denzel and Juanita ask if the experience has given the boys any ideas. Mario suggests that because he is lucky to be gifted in math, maybe he should offer to help some of his friends with their homework two evenings a month. Miguel thinks he'd like to try it with his friends, too, and wonders if there might be a way they could do it so that it would be fun for everyone. Together, they plan a "math helper" ritual in which their family will help some students with math.

chapter 11

Bridging the Gap
Between Generations

One of the sad results of American's fast-changing society has been the decline in communication and understanding between the generations. In years past, it was common for children to live at home until they married. While the trend may be returning to that model somewhat, we are now accustomed to living separately from our families as soon as we have completed high school, or shortly thereafter. Many of us have been raised thousands of miles away from our extended families, visiting them only occasionally. We hardly know those relatives that live far away, and they don't know much about us, either.

One function of family rituals is to countermand this loss. The following activities focus on ways to develop a richer understanding of those we barely know, but are related to and care about, despite the miles between us.

ACTIVITY: Do You Know Me?

The Objective

To encourage greater familiarity between grandchildren and their grandparents.

The Situation

On balance, most children have positive feelings toward their older relatives. But how well do the young members of your family really know the older ones? For example, would your son be able to answer these questions about his grandfather?

> "What is Grandpa's favorite food?"
> "What was the best movie he has seen in the past year?"
> "Would he rather play a sport or watch one?"
> "What political party does he support, and why?"
> "What was his favorite thing to do when he was young?"
> "How did he meet Grandma?"

The older generation has a lot to offer the younger, but those gifts will not be given if they don't know each other well.

Materials Needed

Pencil and notebook, or tape recorder if preferred

☙ ☙ ☙

Tell your children that you are going to hold a ceremony to honor their grandparents. Introduce the idea as follows:

"Each of your grandparents has done a lot for our family, but all of them could be helpful to you kids if you knew them better. They have a lot of information about our extended family, our ancestors, and life in general. The best way to get them to share what they know is to show them that you are interested in their lives. What I propose

is that you decide which grandparent each of you would like to interview for a half an hour or so, just to get to know them better. You should keep notes about what you learn. Then we'll hold a special dinner for them and you can tell the whole family what you have discovered. I think everyone will be interested in what you will have to tell us, even their spouses!"

Although it's best if the children think up their own questions, they may need some help. You can give them the questions just listed; here are some other examples:

"What's the best time you ever had when you were a kid?"
"What's the most embarrassing thing you ever did?"
"What kinds of games did you play when you were young?"
"What was your first job like?"
"What have you done that you are most proud of?"
"What career other than your own would you have liked
  to have had?"
"What would you say is your best trait? Your worst trait?"

When the interviews are done, invite all the relatives you wish to dinner, including of course, the grandparents as guests of honor. Introduce the dinner as a "getting to know them" feast. You might ask the honorees what their favorite foods are and prepare them. At the dinner, use kerosene lamps as the sole lighting, humorously indicating that you are recreating the "olden days." You could also ask the honorees to bring tapes or CDs of the music they loved when they were teenagers. Before the meal, ask your kids to make their presentations, as simply or as fancy as they prefer. Then, during the meal, encourage the grandparents to embellish on the answers they gave in their interviews.

Variation

Repeat the whole procedure for other elders in the family.

ACTIVITY: Portrait of Papa

The Objective

To help grandparents feel that they have contributed to the family and will be remembered for it; to show a tangible act of appreciation and love on the part of the grandchildren toward their grandparents.

The Situation

Many of us who have been blessed with grandparents in our lives remember the stories they told us and look forward to retelling them to our own children and grandchildren. Sad stories, romantic tales, funny incidents from their childhoods, memorized by the listeners through years of hearing them repeated, often with new details added at each telling.

   In order to capture these stories for future generations and to create a thoughtful heirloom for all to share, build a book to give your grandparents that holds all the stories they have told over the years.

Materials Needed

Photo album, journal, or scrapbook; copies of stories printed or written out; photos, if possible

෨ ෨ ෨

Either type and print out or neatly write down the stories that have been repeated many times. Confer with other family members about the details. Have brainstorming sessions to get them down as accurately as possible. Try and add as many details as possible. If you decide to print the stories, you may want to print them out in a large point size—16- to 20-point type—to make them easier for an elderly person to read.

Artfully put the printed stories in an album. If you have photos or other mementos, make copies and add them to the book. Decorate the cover of the book. Give the book a title and a table of contents. For example:

THE UNFORGETTABLE LIVES OF
PAPA BEN AND GRANDMA LEAH LIEBERMAN

1. *The Journey from Austria to America*
2. *The Handsome Redhead Meets the Big-Eyed Beauty*
3. *Sophie Tucker and the Honeymoon Suite*
4. *Glen Miller's Final Journey*
5. *Ira and the Handcuffs*

Gather as many family members as you can, or wait until there is a holiday when many people are around. Present the book to your grandparents with some fanfare—make it an excuse to celebrate, and make them feel special. Have a party!

ACTIVITY: High-Tech Grandma

The Objective
To help bridge the gap between grandchildren and their grandparents by having the grandchild mentor the grandparent.

The Situation
Peter, a precocious twelve-year-old, loves all things electronic and high tech: computers and the Internet, videogames, stereo systems, you name it. His favorite pastime is surfing the Web.

His parents, Julie and Ted, are planning their monthly visit to Grandma Mimi's house in a neighboring town. As much as Peter loves his grandmother, he quickly becomes bored at her house. He complains that "there's nothing to do there."

Mimi realizes that she and Peter, the youngest of her five grand-children, don't know each other as well as she would like. Recently, she has learned that a friend in her book group publishes an e-mail newsletter for her extended family. Mimi loves the idea and would like to develop a newsletter for her own family, but she has never learned how to work on her computer, much as her husband and friends have tried to teach her. She complains that she just has "a block" about electronic equipment, reminding them that she can't program the VCR either!

Materials Needed
Computer, spiral bound notebook for note taking, pen

ఞ ఞ ఞ

When Ted heard about his mother-in-law's frustrations with her com-puter, he immediately saw a chance for both Peter and Mimi to share an opportunity. After all, Peter was already part of a program at his middle school in which elders from their town came into the school once a week and learned computer skills from the students. Peter had been enjoying this work immensely.

He mentioned this to Mimi at dinner and watched her face light up. She suggested that if Peter was willing, she would cook him his fa-vorite meal every Tuesday evening and then they could work together on the computer for a couple of hours.

Peter was enthusiastic for several reasons. He would get to enjoy his grandmother's delicious cooking, he could teach her a valuable skill, and he would be an active participant in the family's newsletter. As the youngest cousin and the only child in his nuclear family, he had often felt left out of some of the extended family's activities. Here was a way that he could be a real contributor.

ACTIVITY: Cousin Cuisine

The Objective

To help cousins of different ages get to know and understand each other better, thus enhancing the family's overall cohesiveness.

The Situation

In many families the range of ages among first cousins can be fairly wide. An individual may well have cousins the same age as his or her parents. Because of the age differences, the cousins probably don't know each other very well. As a result, they miss out on the benefits out of closeness and support that can be part of family relationships.

Materials Needed

Food for a feast

                                 ~~ ~~ ~~

Contact all the cousins in the family and tell them you want to establish a "cousins' feast." Perhaps the best time to do this is when your whole family is planning a reunion anyway. Gather the cousins together in the morning (if there are more than eight of them, you might want to suggest that they form several teams, making sure that they maximize the age spread in each group). The oldest person is the captain of the group. Tell them to plan, shop for, and cook a grand feast that will be attended that evening only by them. They might include dishes that are popular with their various families.

After they have eaten, they take turns, starting with the oldest cousins as models, telling stories about the family's grandparents, aunts, and uncles. These stories are tape-recorded and then transcribed as computer files. These are then e-mailed or mailed to each family and kept for all to read. You might also want to play the tapes sometime during your family reunion, if that is when you hold this ritual.

Variation

Turn this rite into a tradition that you repeat each year, adding new stories to the family record for new generations to read over the years.

ACTIVITY: Senior Counselors

The Objective

To provide counseling by elders to younger family members.

The Situation

Older people are often more patient and have more wisdom than do younger adults. It would seem that elders would make ideal counselors for younger family members who are dealing with life's difficulties. For most situations, the majority of older people are probably equipped with the knowledge and skills that are needed to make them good advisers. There are, however, a myriad of circumstances, such as sexual abuse and serious emotional disturbance, where professional assistance is required.

Therefore, if elders are to make use of their rich experiences in the assistance of their younger relatives, they would do well to obtain some prior training. Training in counseling may be achieved in a number of ways. The best way is to take a course or two at a local college. Videotapes and books on the subject are also available. One of the most important lessons of this training is recognizing when a professional is needed. Once the elder has been adequately prepared, he or she is available to assist with personal and couples' problems.

Materials Needed

None

℘ ℘ ℘

The counseling session between elder and the younger family member takes the form of a ritual. Find a very private place where the session will not be disturbed. Most of the rooms in your house are probably not private enough. A parked car or a long walk in the woods may often serve the purpose admirably. It is important that the counselee feels comfortable with the place. The session begins with both parties facing East, the direction of new beginnings. It is a good idea to open a sachet that gives off a fruity aroma, also symbolizing spring and new starts. The elder introduces the session with words such as these:

"As you know, Emily, I am not a professional counselor. If we find that your concern is beyond my scope, I will recommend that you see someone who is a professional. Now, let me say that I love you and I want to help you. One of the best ways I can help is to assist you in thoroughly describing your situation. That may take several sessions, each lasting no more than one hour. You can help this to work if, between sessions, you will think about the questions I ask you. When we feel we fully understand what is happening, together we will try to find several feasible solutions.

"I'll tell you how you are doing and I honestly want you to do the same for me. For example, if I ask you a question you don't feel comfortable answering, please let me know. Finally, I swear that I will keep everything you say to me as a sacred secret. Okay? Let's start."

If the problem is not too serious, the elder, being a relative, may have advantages over a professional in doing the counseling. For example, she may know a lot about the counselee's background. The elder may be more readily available. Also, the counselee may feel better able to be revealing with a relative rather than a professional.

Obviously, this ritual of counseling is not for every situation, but it can be successful if the elder and the problem situation are a good match.

chapter 12

Healing Illnesses
and Injuries

When people are sick, they often experience negative emotions—fear, sadness, anger. The family feels these emotions, too, as they wait for their loved one's recovery and try to speed it along by giving loving care.

Rituals that are designed to promote healing often rely on symbols to help participants get in touch with feelings they would rather not acknowledge. As ritual expert Nancy Rubin states, "Many rituals are often symbolic rather than direct expressions of strong emotions . . . it is the unspoken message of a ritual that makes it so powerful." A healing ceremony is usually focused on fostering positive thoughts, but may also allow for the release of disruptive emotions, openly or through unspoken symbols. For example, a child might draw a picture of her disease, place it on a pillow, and pound it with her fists, crying, "I hate you! Get out of me!" Thus, you might want to consider providing an outlet for negative feelings, as well as trying to cultivate positive emotions in your plan.

ACTIVITY: Little Gifts

The Objective

To help an ill child recover from sickness-induced depression.

The Situation

Vinny had the flu, and he was miserable. The normally active fifteen-year-old didn't feel like doing anything. He was especially sad because his mom, Coletta, could only be with him part of the day. A single working mother, she could only get away from the small food market she managed for a half an hour at a time. By the third day of his sickness, Vinny was getting depressed.

Materials needed

Items a sick child would enjoy

෨ ෨ ෨

Coletta hoped that maybe if she organized a "Get well, cheer up" ceremony, it would improve her son's spirits. She dipped into her savings and bought him some things she thought he would like: a new computer game, a paperback novel about hockey, and his favorite (expensive) fruit: a papaya, a cantaloupe, and a large mango. When she got home, she found him sleeping. She replaced the objects on the altar they had built together near his bed. She sprayed the room with pine-scented pump disinfectant to get rid of the medicine smell. The pleasant aroma awakened Vinny, and when he saw what was on his altar, he smiled for the first time since he had become ill.

"You know what to do with the computer game and the book," she told him, "but I want you to do something special with the fruit I have bought you. I know you haven't felt much like eating, but I also know you really like papaya, cantaloupe, and mango. I'm going to say a prayer over them now, and I hope they're going to help you feel better.

"Dear God, please give these little gifts of mine the power to cheer Vinny up. He's been feeling sick and he's trying to be very brave about it. I hope you'll bless these gifts for him, so that soon they will help him feel much better."

Coletta hoped that the presents would work as amulets the same way that saying the rosary did for her, so she explained to Vinny her plan: "Over each of the next few days, you are going to start feeling a lot better. I hope you'll enjoy playing the game and reading the book. Also, I've put a knife beside the fruit, so that any time you feel like it, you can eat a slice. When you eat some, I want it to remind you that I love you very much and that I wish I could be home with you all the time. I'm going to continue to pray that God will make these presents magical, so that every time you enjoy one, you get a little better." She could see from his face that this brief a ceremony made Vinny a much happier boy.

ACTIVITY: What Can We Do?

The Objective
To help young children deal with the prolonged illness of a peer.

The Situation
There are times in the lives of our children when friends or other children in the family become ill and need extended care away from home. Although terribly frightening for the afflicted child, this situation can also be frightening for the healthy children who care about the sick child.

Questions inevitably arise about the nature of the sickness, the whereabouts of the sick friend or relative, whether or not the healthy child might also get sick, and whether or not the sick child will die.

Anxiety is heightened when friends and relatives of the ill child are unable to visit the hospital and see for themselves the condition of the sick child.

Materials Needed

Video camera, two unused videotapes, VCR, TV

∾ ∾ ∾

Carol White teaches second grade in a large urban elementary school. One of her students, Emilio Gold, has been hospitalized with spinal meningitis. Although he is out of the pediatric intensive care unit, he is still quite sick. All of the children in the class, and many others in the school, have had to get precautionary injections of gamma globulin, as this is a virulent and serious infection.

The morale in class is low. The children feel frightened for their own health, miss their popular classmate, and are not able to visit him to see for themselves that he is recovering. Ms. White wants to help lift their spirits, but is unsure how.

Carol has been to the hospital to visit Emilio several times since he became sick, taking him cards and notes from his classmates on each visit. Now that he is feeling somewhat better, she can see that he still misses his friends as much as they miss him. She takes him some books and small toys to play with, and asks him how she can help him feel better. Despondently he replies, "I just want to go to school with my friends."

With the help of Emilio's parents, Carol decides to videotape interviews with her class to share with Emilio. The children in Ms. White's class are enthusiastic about the project, too. Carol ties it in with their weekly reading and writing time, so that pairs of two classmates write a brief list of questions and interview each other while a fifth grade helper videotapes the sessions. At the end of the week, the class has an inventive and hilarious videotape for Carol to show Emilio.

Emilio's reaction to the video is even better than Carol and his family could ever have anticipated. He is the happiest they have seen him since he first became sick. It is his idea to videotape his hospital experience for her to take back to the class. Emilio's parents help him write a script that explains his illness for his classmates. It is important to him to assure his friends that the injection they each received will protect them from contracting spinal meningitis.

Emilio's dad, Alan, has helped him formulate questions about his illness and has videotaped Emilio's version of his week in the hospital. Carol takes the tape into school on Monday to share with the other students. Their relief at seeing their classmate sitting up in bed, making faces for their benefit, and introducing them to his many adult visitors, including hospital staff, is touching. The children beg to see it several times throughout the day and over the course of the week.

By the beginning of the next week, the class is back on track, able to concentrate on their second-grade studies and playing happily together. Emilio's return is imminent and everyone is feeling a great sense of anticipation. The class decides to make "Welcome back" posters and have a party upon his return, while viewing the two videotapes one last time.

The videotape made by Emilio served the important function of relieving his friends of their anxiety about his well-being. The class could see for themselves that Emilio was recovering. For young children, it is very comforting to be able to see the surroundings of the sick person, the caregivers, the room, the furnishings, and so on.

For Emilio, the videotape produced for him by his classmates was not only entertaining, but also a great comfort. It allowed him to see his friends in a familiar place, doing the things that he often did with them. It gave him the hope that he would soon be well enough to return to his daily activities.

ACTIVITY: There's Nothing to Fear—We're Here

The Objective
To reduce a child's fear of being in the hospital.

The Situation
Few situations are harder on a family than when a child must go to the hospital to have a serious operation. As well as being afraid and very sick, most children are reluctant to leave their parents. They are worried that they'll feel lonely and miss their family being around them.

Materials Needed
Pump-action spray smelling of spring flowers, huge Teddy bear

Arrange for relatives, including several members of the extended family, if possible, to meet together in the child's hospital room. Spray the room with the scent of spring flowers to make the place feel more cheerful. Speak to the child about how the family wishes for everything to go well for her, and that she will be well looked after by all of the staff of the hospital—the doctors and nurses, and the surgeon, too. All of these people are going to help her feel better, and she will come back to the family after the operation a happy and healthy person. Tell her that although she is away from home, she will not be far from everyone's thoughts and hearts, as everyone will be thinking of her, loving her very much.

Plan in advance for someone to bring an enormous Teddy bear (amulets need not always be small enough to fit into the hand!). Suggest that each member of the family, one by one, go up to Katie and, giving the Teddy bear a big hug, tell her how they will be thinking of her and praying that she will have an easy time of it. Point out that each hug makes the bear more capable of watching over her. Then they each give her a hug and a kiss, too. When everyone has participated, they form a circle around her bed, holding hands, and sing or hum, "When You Walk through a Storm, Hold Your Head Up High." Everyone except her parents then leave the room as a group, blowing her a kiss and saying, "See you soon!"

Variation

Convene a family gathering when the child comes out of hospital to celebrate her having weathered her operation successfully. Then praise her for facing the fears associated with the operation and overcoming them (stress the role that the family's love played in buttressing her ability to do so—that way the family can also share in the celebration). At this celebration bring out a special envelope into which cards that everyone has made have been placed. She can store these away in a safe and special place, from which they can be drawn out again if she ever needs them.

ACTIVITY: We're All with You!

The Objective

To harness the spirit of a family's caring during a parent's illness, through a simultaneous effort to provide emotional support.

The Situation

The serious illness of a parent, especially a mother, is always a stressful time for the children, who find it hard to understand why they are not getting the care they are used to. Being sick is doubly difficult for her, because she worries about her children's welfare, as well as being concerned about the seriousness of her own disease.

Lisa, the mother of two young children, Zach and Trisha, is very ill, but the doctors do not know what is wrong with her. She has had a battery of tests, but she will not hear the results for several days. Lisa is an extremely positive person; she looks for the good in everything and everyone, but even she is having a tough time during this waiting period. She can't help contemplating the "what ifs."

She worries about what's ahead for Zach and Trisha, who are seven and nine. They know she is ill, and the stress of this difficult period is starting to take a toll on all of them. Lisa decides that it's time to step up to the plate and take charge of the situation. But what can she do? She doesn't have any solid information yet. Well, first things first: she needs a boost of positive energy, not only emotionally, to get through this situation, but to help her body and to encourage her children as well. She believes wholeheartedly in the power of positive thinking. She also believes that surrounding herself with people who love her can only have good effects. She decides to tap into these potent sources of energy.

Materials Needed
A telephone

❧ ❧ ❧

Lisa contacts friends and family via telephone—many of the people in her address book. Most of them already know about her mysterious illness; if they don't, she gives a brief explanation. She asks each person if they would set aside two minutes of their time on Thursday night from 8:00 to 8:02 P.M. She wants them to send her their good thoughts/positive energy/prayers—whatever their spiritual beliefs or religious affiliation might call for. She tells them that they will be a part of a large circle of those who care about her, all of whom will be joining to send her family a spiritual message, which will multiply their power exponentially.

So, from 8:00 to 8:02, forty-three friends and members of Lisa's family stop cooking dinner, shut off their television sets or computers, and use whatever method they may choose for getting through to a higher power in an effort to aid Lisa and her family with their struggle. Also at Lisa's request, they have written their words on a sheet of paper. When they have finished reading the words, they set fire to the paper and toss it into the fireplace. If they don't have a fireplace, they take it outside so that the smoke can rise into the air as a symbolic prayer. Lisa and her children try to visualize what these kind folks are doing.

In the minutes after 8 o'clock, Lisa, Zach, and Tricia are amazed to discover that they each experience a powerful sense of being affected by a force they can't describe. Each of them becomes aware of being moved by powerful emotions and realize that they are shedding tears of gratitude.

Variation

You might want to form a positive life force/prayer group in advance of a difficult situation, so that members of the group can call upon the others as a "power supply" when they need it. You could use the power of a group of mutual friends as well as members of the family. Such a group could decide to gather together, or stay separate, or a combination of both—whatever is convenient for everyone.

ACTIVITY: All Together Now

The Objective

To relieve family members of the stress of caring for sick or elderly relatives by sharing the responsibility.

The Situation

Marco and Diana are teenagers attending high school. One day, their parents, Tina and Ric, announce at dinner that their maternal uncle, Xavier, who has multiple sclerosis and who lives nearby, has become much worse and will need close attention, probably for the rest of his life. Hiring professional help is not feasible or practical at this point.

Tina and Ric make it clear to the teens that it will not be possible for them to be the only caregivers, since they both work full-time and Ric has an additional part-time job. Their expectation is that Diana and Marco will take on some of the care of their uncle.

Materials Needed

None

After the family's weekly Sunday dinner, they gather in the living room to discuss the state of Uncle Xavier's affairs. In order to be fair to everyone, the family divides the chores among themselves according to their availability and skill level. For example, Ric drives through his brother-in-law's neighborhood every Tuesday and Thursday evening on his way to his part-time job. It is easy for him to drop off a dinner cooked by Diana on those evenings. Marco has his driver's license, and, since he will do anything to drive the car, volunteers to take his uncle to his weekly doctor appointments after school. Marco is proud that he is strong enough to support his uncle's weight as he enters and exits the car. He can also maneuver Xavier's wheel-chair in and out of the trunk more easily than can others in his family.

Ric and Marco spend time on Saturday afternoons doing some of the heavier chores and yard work at Xavier's small home, while Diana and her mom do the lighter housework and help Xavier pay his bills. When the work is done, they all go to the early Mass together at the Catholic Church just down the street. They return to Uncle Xavier's for a light dinner, usually take-out. Frequently, Marco and Diana have Saturday evening plans, but Tina and Ric will stay at Xavier's for a video or a game of cards until he grows weary. On Sundays, Xavier's parents are able to visit him, although since they are quite elderly, their ability to help him is limited.

In just over a year, it becomes necessary for Xavier to enter an assisted living situation in a nearby suburb. Diana and Marco, who were at first reluctant to give up so much of their free time, have grown fond of their uncle and of the time they have spent with him over the previous year. The family decides to continue their Saturday afternoons with Xavier even though his circumstances have changed. The teens now both feel that the time with their favorite uncle is invaluable, and they wouldn't think of giving it up.

ACTIVITY: Cards with Nana

The Objective
To help children visit a sick relative or friend who needs comforting.

The Situation
Edna is eighty-one years old and has cancer. Her husband has been dead for eight years, but her youngest daughter Tracey and her family live near the hospital where she has recently been admitted. She has

been in the hospital for almost two weeks and finds it lonely and depressing. Although Tracey and her family come often to visit her, it is hard for her grandchildren to see their "Nana," usually so spirited, now sick and in the hospital.

The grandchildren, Jamie, nine, and Samantha, twelve, don't like going to the hospital to visit because they don't know what to say to their Nana. They answer her questions politely but have little to offer beyond the usual pleasantries. Nana can see their awkwardness and doesn't know how to help. Sensing that she doesn't have long to live, she desperately wants to be with her grandchildren, but understands their discomfort.

Materials Needed
Board games, cards, any activity that the sick person would enjoy teaching and playing with visitors

꙰ ꙰ ꙰

Tracey understands the situation well, since the family has already experienced the death of her father. The children were much younger then, but Tracey remembers feeling tongue-tied and uncomfortable herself when visiting her dad. Because he had had a series of debilitating strokes, it was much more difficult to interact with him in the end than it is with her mother.

Tracey decides that instead of taking flowers or balloons to the hospital, they will take a deck of cards. It is clear to her that her mother doesn't have much time left, and she really wants her children to have a chance to get to know their only living grandmother. Both of her children love to play cards, and Edna is a real whiz. Tracey asks her mom if she will teach Jamie and Samantha how to play bridge.

Edna is delighted, as this is her favorite game, and she misses terribly the biweekly game she used to play with her friends.

Samantha is a quick study and loves the game. Jamie learns more slowly and requires everyone's patience, but learns to enjoy the game after several sessions. As they play cards, the children begin to talk with Edna about their lives—the sports they play, their school days, and their friends. They frequently stay for her dinnertime and sometimes an early TV show before leaving for the evening. Samantha and Jamie are surprised and thrilled to learn that their Nana loves some of their favorite programs, too.

After two weeks, Edna is moved to a nursing home. She and her grandchildren have formed a special bond that they didn't have before. The children are relaxed and comfortable at her bedside, and are able to talk easily with her about many things that interest them all. They try other games, but everyone realizes that such pastimes really aren't necessary. Tracey is thrilled with the new relationship, realizing that as her mother gets sicker, the children will be able to be with her and give her true comfort.

chapter 13

Honoring Departed Family Members

Although a funeral ritual or memorial service is almost always held soon after a loved one dies, often this is just the beginning of the grieving process. Frequently, family members are still in shock, unable to cope with the enormity of their sadness at the time of a funeral. Rituals that occur several weeks or months later or that are held annually to honor and remember a deceased loved one are healing events, meant to celebrate the life of the person taken from our midst.

ACTIVITY: The Loss of Milo

The Objective
To help a child grieve the loss of his or her pet and to prepare for future deaths in the family.

The Situation
In general, Western society does not attach much significance to the death of a pet. Frequently, neighbors, close friends, and relatives are

not even aware that the family pet has died. Nevertheless, the death of a pet is almost always a significant event to a family, especially to the children. A pet's death is often the first death a child must face.

Materials Needed

Soft cloth for a shroud, shoebox or appropriately sized box for the pet's body, the pet's toys or food bowl, flowers for the gravesite, candles that are the same color as your pet's fur, a stone marker, paint or chalk for the marker.

ஸ் ஸ் ஸ்

Lindsey is an eight-year-old girl who has loved Milo, the cat, with all her heart since she was a toddler. Milo is almost twice Lindsey's age and is clearly beginning to fail. As Milo's health continues to worsen, Lindsey's parents begin to explain death and dying.

Lindsey's mother, Jennie, cuddles up with her in her cozy bed and reads her a story about the loss of a pet. Although Lindsey does not completely understand the concept of death, she begins to ask questions about it. Jennie also explains to Lindsey what happens at a funeral.

Within a few weeks, Milo's kidneys fail, and the family decides to have Milo euthanized so that he will not have to suffer. Lindsey is devastated by his death.

Coping with death is an individual and personal activity. Since Milo was an integral part of the family, it makes it that much harder. Lindsey's parents want her to see that it is normal to grieve over the loss of a pet. They believe that being completely open and honest about their feelings of sorrow over Milo's death is the best way to help Lindsey understand that grieving is healthy.

Lindsey's parents have worked closely with her to design an appropriate funeral for Milo. The veterinarian has given the family Milo's body so that they can bury him in the backyard. Lindsey and her mom sew a simple flannel shroud for him, and Jennie puts the wrapped body in a large cardboard shoebox. The family joins together at Milo's burial site, with each member lighting a candle that is the same color as Milo's fur, as a sort of homage to him. As they do so, Lindsey's father says a short prayer aloud. They lower the box into the ground, and Lindsey places a tuft of Milo's fur from his brush and his water dish on top of the box. After filling in the hole, they reminisce about Milo's antics. Lindsey has picked some flowers for the gravesite and chosen a large stone as a grave marker. She draws his name on the stone with chalk, and will paint his name at another time. After the funeral, Lindsey draws several pictures of her memories with Milo. Jennie sticks them on the fridge to help gain a sense of closure. She also finds several snap-shots of Milo to put in magnetic frames, also for the refrigerator door.

Over the next few weeks, the family reads Lindsey's favorite books by Cynthia Rylant, *Dog Heaven* and *Cat Heaven*. It is most comforting for her to think of her beloved kitty in such a special, ani-mal-friendly place. At their family meeting, they say a little prayer for Milo, and Lindsey lights a candle of memory for him and places it in front of her favorite picture of Milo, asleep in a stroller with her when she was a baby.

Variation

The family observes Pet Memorial Day (the second Sunday in September) by placing fresh flowers on the grave.

ACTIVITY: Sharing Our Grief

The Objective

To make it possible for all the members of the family to participate in honoring the life of the deceased member.

The Situation
In many families, the members live considerable distances from each other. It is often difficult for everyone to gather for the funeral services of a family member who has died. In such cases, it may be necessary to hold simultaneous services in the homes of those who cannot make it.

Materials Needed
Speakerphones for each location, favorite food and music of the deceased

      ◈ ◈ ◈

In order for everyone to participate in the service for a deceased member of the family, the telephone system can be a great aid. At a preset time a conference call is placed to each of the homes of the family's members. Not everyone can afford a speakerphone, but it should be possible to borrow one from work or from a friend.

Prior to the service, each family cooks some food that was especially enjoyed by the deceased, so that the cooking aromas permeate the rooms in all the homes in which the service is being held. Also, at the prescribed time, each group begins playing the favorite music of the deceased person, agreed upon in advance. Perhaps someone could make copies of the departed person's favorite song and everyone could sing it. As the service begins, all the lights in the rooms are turned on, and the participants face the North, the direction associated with honoring the dead. You might want to explain that this is the traditional orientation of ceremonies designed to show our love for the deceased.

The most senior member of the family reads a prayer or a poem of love and remembrance to honor the memory of the person who has gone. Any member of the family who wants to say something about the deceased now has a chance to do so. Finally, the senior family member evokes the blessings of all the departed members of the family on all those who remain, by saying,

"In recognizing our loss today, we mean to do honor to all the members of our family who have gone before us. We will keep them in our prayers, and we hope that they will keep us in their hearts."

Variation

If you find that you liked the ceremony, you may want to turn it into tradition. Every year on the anniversary of the person's death, a similar long-distance service may be held.

ACTIVITY: Past, Present, and Future

The Objective

To pay homage to a departed family member who has left life much too quickly, and to help the family feel "complete" despite losing a key member.

The Situation

Frances Testani, fifty-three, the mother of three grown children and grandmother of six youngsters, has passed away after becoming afflicted by a virulent form of cancer. The whole family is upset. Since Frances died so young and so quickly, they did not have time to say their good-byes properly. After all of the formal funeral arrangements have taken place, her oldest daughter Joan decides that the family should hold their own special ceremony. She wants this ritual to be more personal than the funeral and to contrast with the standardized formal practices so it can be truly meaningful to each member of the family.

Materials Needed

A large rug, a collection of family pictures, a large square of cardboard, glue

୶ ୶ ୶

Frances' family gathers on a pleasant day at a place that was sacred to Frances, her backyard rose garden. A large rug has been arranged on the ground near the garden's gate and the family members have organized themselves around it. Frances' husband John stands and steps onto the rug. In the center of the rug for all to see, he props up a montage of pictures taken of Frances and her family over the years, cemented to a large piece of cardboard. He says, "I represent our family's past and our beloved Frances' part in it." He shares his memories about each of the pictures and speaks about what Frances has meant to his life.

Now Frances' oldest daughter, Kim, steps into the center of the circle beside her father, and says, "I want to speak about the present. What would Mom want us to do now? Can't you just hear her answer to this question? 'Love each other, take care of each other, and make sure your dad is okay!' In the weeks, month and years to come, I think the best thing we can do to honor Mom's memory is to try real hard to remember these three rules. Does anybody else want to share their ideas about what she would want from us now?"

Her son Pat speaks up: "It seems to me that now there is a hole in the family that nobody can fill. We are all going to have to remember that it is more important than ever to stick together and be united. This is what she wanted. She has kept us all together. Now each person must contribute toward making sure the glue remains strong."

Last of all, Frances' son Ed steps onto the rug and says, "My task is to talk about the future. What do we do to make certain that Mom can live on in the actions of everyone who has loved her? Well, as we all know, she hated that damned cancer. She always thought that if she tried hard enough, she could fix anything, but she couldn't fix that. Nevertheless, it seems to me there is something that we can do about it. I suggest that we all work hard on a drive to get funds for the American Cancer Society and donate them in Mom's name. What do you say we all get together and see how much money we can get our friends and the other members of our family to donate to this important cause?"

In this ritual, the family strives to deal with past, present, and future in a way that would celebrate their lost one's life. When it is over, they all agree that they have achieved some relief from their unbearable grief, that they have been able to do something positive about a situation that had seemed totally negative to them all.

Variation

Each year the family plans to get together in the same spot that the first gathering took place, not on the actual date that Frances died, but on the anniversary of this ritual. They will think again about the past, present, and future of the family, and as time passes, they will surely find that, more and more, this becomes a joyful occasion.

ACTIVITY: The Death of a Teen

The Objective

To help the family and friends of the victims grieve together, beyond the traditional funeral service.

The Situation

We see it over and over again in the local and national news. A teenager dies an untimely death in a car accident, often after drinking too much. Tragically, several teens may die in the same accident, leaving their community of family and friends bereft.

In many of these sad situations where alcohol or drugs are involved, friends of the victim feel an overwhelming sense of guilt for having allowed their friend to drive. "If only I had said something," they think, "T. J. would be here with me today."

Materials Needed

For the accident site: Flowers, balloons, other mementos that remind friends of the victims; for the memorial cookout: A large tray, two dozen or more votive candles, matches, framed photographs of the victim

∾ ∾ ∾

Many high schools and universities have a support system of grief counselors already in place to deal with a crisis such as the sudden death of a student. If your community does not, it is essential that you speak to the authorities and make certain that counselors are available immediately following a death.

Fellow students, family, and friends often congregate at the site of a fatal crash to memorialize the victim with flowers, poetry, song lyrics, balloons, photographs, and stuffed animals. Encourage this in your community, as it bonds the group and supports the kind of healing grief that is necessary.

Help organize a memorial service for the victim at a place where he or she liked to be: a baseball diamond, a bowling alley, your backyard pool, a nearby state park. This could occur several weeks or months after the funeral and might serve as an occasion to raise money for a cause the victim cared about. Try to keep the mood light initially by having a cookout and a focusing activity such as a softball game, swimming, or touch football.

After everyone has had a chance to relax and has eaten, gather in a protected area where a makeshift altar (it could be as simple as a picnic table) has been set up with pictures of the victim and a tray of unlit votive candles. Lead the group by describing a special memory you have of the victim, and ask if others would please now share their memories. As each participant states a memory, light one of the votive candles, or have him or her light a candle. After all have had the opportunity to express themselves, recite a brief poem and ask for a moment of silence. If you are fundraising, this would be the time to ask for donations.

Variation
The memorial picnic could become an annual event for as long as the friends are in high school or university together.

ACTIVITY: Happy Birthday to You

The Objective
To create an occasion to celebrate the life of a departed family member or close friend. This can be an opportunity to impart deeper meaning about the significance of life. For example, even though family members pass away, they can still be with us in spirit, during this family rite and always.

The Situation
Birthdays are typically a time when we have an opportunity to celebrate the life of a family member or friend. When people die, though,

families tend to stop celebrating their birthdays.

Last year, Bill Stimson passed away after a long battle with cancer. He left two young children, Joe and Pete, and a wife, Carolyn. Among his three brothers and sisters, Bill was known as the "life of the party." Every summer at the beginning of June, for his birthday, he would host a large family barbecue, always including his mother, his brothers and sisters, and their entire families.

These parties were characterized by huge plates of appetizers, steak tips from his favorite steak restaurant that he cooked on the grill, and cakes from the bakery where he used to go as a child. After everyone had eaten, he would organize a touch football game that most of the family joined in, although he never played himself. Bill preferred to stand on the sidelines of the game and coach each team to victory, switching his team allegiance just when it seemed that one team was on its way to victory—he loved to cheer for the underdog.

Materials Needed

Party supplies including food, drink, and activities that will remind the invitees of the departed family member

        ~ ~ ~

This year, as Bill's birthday approached, the party planning that used to go on during May and early June seemed conspicuously absent, which was getting everyone down. One day, when Carolyn was talking to Bill's sister Andrea, she suggested that the family go ahead and have Bill's annual birthday celebration anyway, as a tribute to him and his memory. When Carolyn called up the family members to invite them over for the tribute party, she was pleasantly surprised to find that everyone was eager and excited to make it a special day, volunteering to pick up the steak tips and other supplies and to help out in any way.

When the day of the party came, the family started to interact with each other the way they would have ordinarily, although topics of conversation were focused around Bill and his memory. In fact, as different people went about operating the grill or setting up the appetizer trays, they found it hard to refrain from saying things like, "This is the way that Bill always set up the trays," or "We have to wait to play football until after we eat the cakes; that's how your dad would have done it. . . ."

After the football game the family gathered on the front porch of the house. Because he had so loved to sit on a bench on a beautiful spot overlooking the river in their town, the family had decided to get flower bulbs and miniature trees that they knew Bill would favor. Each person revealed what bulbs or saplings they had gotten for Bill. Everyone helped to dig in the plants before returning to the house to continue the game and eat a piece of cake.

If you like this service, here are some other ideas about what you might use as gifts for the birthday party of a deceased person:

- *Toys for tots whose parents are poor*
- *Plantings for the local golf course*
- *Contributions to a political campaign or some other group that the deceased believed strongly in*
- *Gifts that would have made the deceased person laugh*
- *Some object that would make life easier for the deceased person's spouse.*

Variation

This activity might take place annually on the birthday of the person who has passed away, becoming a family tradition.

ACTIVITY: Our Favorite Place

The Objective

To honor the bond a deceased loved one nurtured while he or she was still alive.

The Situation

Grandpa loved to go fishing. He took the grandchildren to his favorite stream in the woods behind his home to teach them to fish. When the grandchildren turned four or five, he would buy them their first fishing poles. He took time and care teaching them about the pole, how to put the bait on the hook, and then to cast. It was one of his favorite activities. The grandchildren loved it, also. Even though some of them didn't particularly care to fish, they all loved going with him to the stream. He was such a lovable guy.

Actually, fishing was a guise for just getting to spend time with Grandpa. That time together was about learning so many different things. When the kids were with him, the love just overflowed from him. They felt safe, and nothing else mattered.

Now, Grandpa has died. Those special times with him are greatly missed. The grandchildren have been talking a lot about "the old times" and have decided to plan a day to remember Grandpa.

Materials Needed

Fishing gear, sign (created in advance)

❧ ❧ ❧

The grandchildren have been talking and have decided to have a "Let's Fish Day." This will be a day where they will bring all their fishing gear, pack a lunch, and go to Grandpa's favorite stream. Uncle Joe now lives in Grandpa's home. Judi, the oldest grandchild, will be contacting him to arrange the date. Some of the grandkids live out of state, so Judi will be contacting them to let them know about this celebration.

The big day arrives. All of the grandchildren are here with fishing gear in tow. Joe joins them, and early in the afternoon on a Saturday, they all walk together down the winding path through the woods to the stream. Along the way they talk about the adventures they shared in these woods with Grandpa. They remember the fort built over by the big pine tree. They remember the patch of very soft grass where they would lie down and look up at the trees, trying to catch a glimpse of the sky. So many wonderful memories flood their minds and conversation.

As the group gets closer to the stream, Kenny announces that he has crafted a sign that reads, "Grandpa's Place." It has a picture of Grandpa, is signed "With much love," and has all the grandchildren's names on it.

One of the things they remember most about this spot is that Grandpa had made a bench and placed it at the elm tree, which sat on a small hillock overlooking the fishing hole. It was still there. The sign that Kenny had made was placed on that elm tree, over the bench. The grandchildren gather around the tree for a moment of silence. Joyce reads a poem she wrote for the occasion.

Soon, several of the young men and women are fishing, while others wade in the knee-deep water. It's just like old times! Before they are ready to leave, they stop and take a moment to thank Grandpa for all of the wonderful memories. They walk, quietly joking about Grandpa and his wry wit, back to Uncle Joe's for the cookout they have prepared in advance.

chapter 14

Dealing with Emergencies

We often hear it said that "a crisis brings out the best in people." That's what we would all like to think, but studies show that emergencies evoke the best *and* the worst, depending on the person. Most people are at their best only when they have strong emotional supports—a loving spouse, close friends, a cohesive family. This is true whether the emergency is local (a fire next door), regional (loss of power in part of the state), national (an oil embargo), or universal (international war).

Rituals encourage cohesion in the family. They can also be used to confront the specific crisis itself, by helping family members:

- *Become aware of their unconscious emotional reactions*
- *Learn that they are not alone in their concerns*
- *Brainstorm possible family plans and choose the best one*
- *Support each other in carrying out the plan.*

Families that are able to act effectively together during an emergency serve as excellent models for everyone.

ACTIVITY: Which Way Out?

The Objective

To help families become more aware of the danger of fire, to devise a strategy for escaping safely in the event of a fire, and to alleviate the fears children may have of fire.

The Situation

Two occurrences in the same week in the lives of the Lenox family made Liam and Tom realize that they needed to discuss fire emergency with their children, Michaela, four, and Colin, six. The first incident was when Michaela came home from daycare one day, excitedly talking about a visit to her daycare center from Engine #14 and several firemen. The fact sheet the firemen had given her to take home recommended that families have an escape plan carefully worked out in case of an emergency. Tom and Liam hadn't wanted to scare their young children in the past, but now recognized that having a plan was the best security they could offer them.

The second incident was when an elderly couple in the neighborhood had experienced a fire in their second-floor apartment, and although they had escaped with only minor smoke inhalation, their three cats had been killed and their apartment destroyed. Colin and Michaela were very sad about the kitties they fondly remembered, and were having nightmares that their apartment might burn, also.

Materials Needed

None

❧ ❧ ❧

One Saturday evening, Liam and Tom sat down with Colin and Michaela over a huge bowl of popcorn, and talked about how disturbing their neighbors' fire had been to all of them. They openly discussed the children's fears with them, answering all of their "what if" questions as they arose.

Next, the four walked together through their large apartment, looking for all the ways they were already fire-safe. Tom pointed out that they were careful not to use too many extension cords and that all the extension cords were in good repair and not winding under carpets. Colin pointed out the smoke detectors and covered his ears as they checked to be sure that each one was in working order. Michaela showed them where the fire extinguishers were and was able to explain how to use a small one, thanks to the firemen's visit the previous week. The family discussed the safe use of matches, where a safe place in the kitchen was for potholders (not too close to the stove), and to be careful not to put paper or cloth too close to light bulbs.

Next, Liam carefully outlined what to do in case of a fire in their home. They designed an escape route, and they practiced the routine several times. The fire department had supplied a comprehensive sheet for families to follow, and Liam used these guidelines.

Michaela and Colin felt more secure after the family's walk-through and discussion. They liked the idea of keeping their shoes and a small flashlight next to their beds, and Michaela said the flashlight would make her feel safe when she had a bad dream—even though she had a nightlight, too!

Tom suggested that at the beginning of each new season, the family incorporate their fire drill and the walk-through routine into their family ritual time. The children loved the idea and asked that popcorn please be included as part of the ritual every time they repeat it!

Variation

Since Michaela and Colin spend every other weekend at their mother's home, Liam and Tom asked her if she would consider conducting a similar ritual with the children so that they would feel fire safe at her home, too. She was happy to do so, and was impressed by how much the children knew about fire safety. A great lover of popcorn, she was glad the children insisted on it at the ritual!

ACTIVITY: Emergency Quiz

The Objective

To help children of any age learn how to deal with the tragedies and emergencies that they might encounter some day.

The Situation

Many children are prepared for the more common emergencies—how to call 911 and at which neighbor's house to meet if forced out of their home. But there are more problems, unusual emergencies that this level of knowledge just doesn't cover. Fires, floods, terrorism, storms, physical threats and injury, school violence—the list goes on and on. Sometimes children think erroneously that they can handle these kinds of problems on their own, too. What is needed is a detailed plan to handle almost any emergency.

Materials Needed

Paper, pencil

෩ ෩ ෩

This ritual helps prepare a family to handle serious crises in a variety of situations. To avoid unnecessarily frightening the children, try to carry it out in a nonthreatening situation. Pick a pleasant sunny morning, preferably a warm summer day, and meet in the room in your house in

Emergency Action Questionnaire

Crisis Situation: (for example, a blizzard) _____

On a separate piece of paper, write out your answers to the following questions:

1. Who do we all call if we become separated from one another? (It is probably wise to call someone such as the children's grandparents if they live far enough away so as not to be affected by whatever crisis you're dealing with.)

2. Where is our family meeting place if this problem occurs?

3. Who are the people you can trust if you are out of contact with our family when this happens?

4. What action should you take if you are injured in this situation?

5. What kind of materials should we keep in the house in case this kind of emergency should occur?

6. Are there any books, articles, or videotapes that can help us to prepare for this type of difficulty? Might there be something on the Internet that would be useful?

7. Is there anyone we know who could give us some good advice about how to deal with a problem like this?

8. Can we design a ritual in advance that we can use when we find ourselves faced with this kind of crisis?

which a number of windows can be opened to the fresh outdoor aromas. Play some soothing music and put some pleasant-smelling flowers in the room. Use your most serene and reassuring voice.

Sit down with your children and ask them to help you draw up a list of all the emergencies and tragedies that they might encounter. Their input is vital in this process. When they have finished brainstorming, add to the list those things that you feel they have overlooked, but are essential. This list should include items that differ according to age. For example, small children may have listed concerns such as threats from strangers and playing with matches, whereas older children may mention school violence, drunk driving, and drugs. The whole family could be threatened by storms, floods, and their attending power outages.

Once a list has been complied, make up a quiz with questions that apply to emergencies in general. The answers will vary with each type of crisis. It might look like the questionnaire on page 187.

When the form is designed, stop working for now. This sort of thinking can be a strain for children, especially the younger ones. A little later, gather the family to fill out a separate questionnaire for each of the situations on your list.

Variation
From time to time, take out one of the questionnaires and use it as a pop quiz. You might want to make a contest out of answering the questions, giving the easier questions to younger children.

ACTIVITY: Helping Our Neighbors

The Objective
To reconnect those who are disconnected from society so that they will be safe during a crisis.

The Situation

The Ramirez family feels well prepared for emergencies, such as an extended period without electricity due to a hurricane, which frequently occur in their area of northern Florida. Although they are ready for several weeks of life without electricity, central heat and air conditioning, or fresh water, they noticed that many of their neighbors and friends, particularly the elderly, are not.

Marina Ramirez, fifteen, wonders if homeless shelters would be able to accommodate their city's homeless population in a time of crisis. Hector, her seventeen-year-old brother, is concerned about how ill prepared people are, too. With the help of their parents, the Ramirez children decide to help their neighborhood with an organized effort to handle a crisis before it is too late.

Materials Needed

None

෴ ෴ ෴

One Sunday evening, as part of their regularly scheduled spiritual time together, the Ramirezes list all of the people in the neighborhood who might need extra help during a blackout, a flood, or some other kind of community-wide emergency. In addition to neighbors, Hector thinks of three homeless people known to frequent the blocks closest to their home. The family lights a candle for each individual or family they think of, and say a prayer in unison for these people's needs.

Marina and her mom visit the nearest homeless shelter, a large one that serves the whole city. They learn that the shelter has enough food to last three or four days and a generator in the event of a blackout, but nonperishable food as well as warm clothing are always welcome. Hector discovers that the elderly and housebound neighbors closest to them need many of the same things as the homeless, with the addition of flashlights, extra batteries, and candles.

Marina and Hector organize a food and clothing drive at their church and are amazed by the generosity of their faith community. Within a few weeks, they are able to accommodate the needs outlined by the shelter and those of their neighbors, too. Additionally, several members of their church, including the Ramirezes, have offered to take in elderly neighbors in the event of a citywide crisis. This is a great relief to those in need and those who lack the support of other family or friends close by.

At the end of the drive, the Ramirez family invites all those who have contributed to a prayer vigil at their home. More than fifty people crowd their small home, lighting candles and praying out loud for the support of divine comfort during an emergency. The feeling of love and camaraderie in the room is overwhelming for all who attend. Hector and Marina know that they have helped many to feel safe and secure in the event of a crisis.

ACTIVITY: Civil Rights Attack

The Objective
To help children deal with racist and other types of prejudice.

The Situation
Americans are increasingly seeing reports of violence and aggression in the schools. To make matters worse, many parents and other influential adults are so overworked that they may feel that they lack the resources to deal with a crisis when it does occur.

Jamal, twelve, attends a small middle school in a suburban town. Although his school experiences have been very positive thus far, a group of older students from the high school have begun to hang out at the elementary school and create problems for some of the students there, calling certain students names and making ethnic and religious slurs.

Last week, a number of older students started to pick on several African American children who were on their way home from school, calling them names and using obscenities. One of Jamal's closest friends was the target of this attack. Although Jamal was not directly involved in the incident, he is African American, and he has developed feelings of anxiety about walking to and from school by himself.

Materials Needed

One large candle, a simple necklace made of blue beads

       ⚭   ⚭   ⚭

Jamal's family gathers together in the evening after the incident occurs. The ritual they are holding includes members of the immediate family, and they have invited several members of the community, including other students, parents, and teachers to participate. The group gathers in a circle around a large candle, which they light as a symbol of their unity against ignorance and violence. Jamal's father asks him a number of questions about how he feels as he walks to and from school. The boy makes it clear how threatened he feels.

His father then asks the people present to join hands and visualize this situation that Jamal so fears. He carefully describes Jamal's ideal journey to school, one on which the youngster walks with a big smile on his face, brimming with confidence. Jamal's dad asks all present to say a prayer that this vision will come true for him.

After this experience, Jamal's mother shows him a necklace she has made from blue beads, which she tells him symbolizes peace as well as his family's strength, a power that will be supporting him every time he journeys to and from school. Each member of the group takes a turn holding the necklace, blessing it with wishes for Jamal's serenity and safety. The ceremony closes with each person giving Jamal an encouraging hug.

Variation

If one of your children is anxious about school, it is likely that any other children you have may be frightened, too. You could alter this ceremony for each of them in several ways. For example, the group-strength necklaces might be made of different colors: red for conflict resolution, green for serenity, white for hope.

ACTIVITY: Bonds of Love

The Objective

To help families who are experiencing anxiety to cope with potential school violence.

The Situation

For the past six years, a new rite of spring has blossomed in the nation's school systems—the unsettling sound of gunshots in the schools. This new phenomenon doesn't have a specific geographic location—it has hit both rural and urban schools, affluent suburban and depressed inner city schools, in all four corners of our nation. Students crying and hugging one another as their injured classmates are carried out of school on stretchers has become a common sight on the national news, as the media exploits the raw emotions of the people involved in the latest tragedy.

An environment where parents once felt relatively safe dropping their children off has now become a calculated risk. If there isn't an actual shooting, there remains the threat of one, because copycat attempts are also happening nationwide. When word leaks out that a school has received a threat, some children do not attend school for days, while others go to school with a tremendous amount of anxiety and fear, clearly not ready to face the task of getting an education.

Many schools have thought long and hard over what to do if a violent event does occur. Various evacuation plans, "lock-down" scenarios, and crisis action plans have been experimented with. Unfortunately, although many schools have trained their faculty on what to do in a crisis situation, many of the parents and students have been left in the dark.

Materials Needed

Floating candles, large bowl of water, jewelry that has meaning to your family's faith, such as a gold cross (used here), a Star of David, chalice

          ❧ ❧ ❧

Tim and Faith have two daughters, Anna and Sadie. Both are students of the Kenmore Public School System—Anna is a ninth grader and her younger sister, Sadie, is a sixth grader. Gradually, it came to Faith's attention that Sadie was not sleeping or eating well. Fearing an eating disorder, Faith made an appointment with the doctor for the following day.

Upon Sadie's evaluation by the doctor, it was determined that there was nothing physically wrong with her. Dr. Rush then started talking to Sadie about school because he had a child in the sixth grade as well. Sadie, when asked questions about school, either would not answer or would change the subject. Dr. Rush and Sadie's mother found this awkward and surprising because Sadie was an honor student and had always looked forward to school and to eventually joining Anna at the high school.

When Sadie and her mother returned home, Anna and Tim had dinner ready—fettucine Alfredo, Sadie's favorite. Sadie sat down to dinner but barely touched her meal. By coincidence, Anna had read in the newspaper about a high school in a neighboring town that had suspended classes for the rest of the week because of a bomb threat. Anna stated that she was nervous going to school because of what she had read and because of what other students were saying about recent shootings in California. One of the rumors she had heard was that her school was next. Anna spoke openly of her fears of being shot. Suddenly, much to the surprise of her family, Sadie burst into tears, sobbing, "I don't want Anna to die! What if someone shoots me? Just because it's always been in high schools so far doesn't mean my stupid school won't be the first middle school to get hit!" She ran from the table, crying convulsively.

Everything seemed clear now. Sadie, only eleven, was terrified of a school shooting in her town. She was afraid not only for herself, but also for her sister and their friends. Tim and Faith took immediate action with their family.

Faith and Anna went to Sadie's room, which she shared with Anna, and comforted her gently and lovingly. Anna talked quietly to her sister about how rumors rarely come true, and even though she did feel afraid sometimes, most often her school felt very safe. Anna explained that the school administration had a Crisis Action Plan that had been shared with the student body. Faith said she would contact the high school principal the next morning to obtain a copy of the plan so that Sadie and her family could read it and learn how to cope with a school emergency. When the girls' father heard of the Crisis Action Plan, he said that every family needed to know about it, and suggested that it be made available to all families in the district. He also thought the school guidance department should develop a list for parents that outlined behaviors in children that might be considered at risk for perpetrating school violence.

It was Anna's idea to perform a spontaneous family ritual to help Sadie through this difficult time. Anna had everyone meet in their family room where she had lit four floating candles in a large bowl of water. After having the family join hands and relax in a moment of centering silence, Anna removed from around her neck the simple gold cross that her grandmother had given her for her confirmation the year before. At the time of her confirmation, Anna's grandmother had said that the cross symbolized strength and would give her the courage to face the years ahead, both the fun times and the strenuous ones. Anna smiled when she gave it to Sadie. "Sadie, I love this cross, and someday I want it back, but right now you need the courage and love that comes with it. While you are wearing the cross, you will have the strength of our whole family behind you. Remember that it will bring you the power to overcome your fears about being shot in school." Their parents each said a prayer for Sadie and Anna, and then the family recited their favorite prayer together, one that Anna had read at her confirmation ceremony.

Although there is still a little anxiety occasionally, Sadie is able to eat normally, sleep regularly, and perform her studies in school. Faith and Tim are proud of Anna's support of her sister, and grateful that the ritual has worked so well.

ACTIVITY: Because We Care

The Objective

Most people feel the need to do *something* when tragedy strikes, but often they feel uncertain about the right thing to do. This ritual is designed so that anyone can do something that will be appreciated.

The Situation

Although the day had started out sunny, by noon a line of menacing clouds had begun moving toward this small midwestern town. She knew that the weather report called for storms, but Joan Karouac couldn't help feeling uneasy about the look of the sky as she drove to pick up her daughter, Linda, from kindergarten. As the afternoon wore on, the feeling in the air became more ominous. At 3 P.M., Joan was greatly relieved to see the bus from the middle school pull up to the corner where she and Linda waited for her other two children, Susan, twelve, and Tim, ten. As she walked the children back to the house, she realized that the clouds had gotten even darker, and had taken on a ghastly yellow tint.

Joan had never experienced weather conditions like these before, so as soon as she was in the house, she turned on the radio. The announcer was saying, ". . . report. In the next half-hour, we are expecting very high winds and heavy rain, with the possibility of tornadoes. The state weather office has recommended that everyone immediately take refuge in the safest place they can find." Joan grabbed the portable phone and quickly ushered her family into the cellar. She called her husband George at his office, but the line was busy.

Within a matter of minutes, she thought she heard the sound she dreaded most: a dull roar like a distant train. The sound rapidly intensified, and her two youngest children began to cry. Holding the three children close, she tried to comfort them with her words, but it was difficult to be heard. Now there was not only the deafening sound of a tornado nearby, but also the racket of objects slamming against the side of her house. Speaking as loudly as she could, she urged the children to say the Lord's Prayer with her.

Before they could even begin to say the prayer, the howl of the storm started to abate. Within moments, everything quieted to an eerie silence. Joan realized that her face was soaked in tears, which she quickly wiped away. The lights in the cellar began to flicker and then went out. Before they did, she was able to find the portable phone. Feeling with her fingers, she called her husband again and this time got through. "My God, Joan, is everyone all right?" asked George.

"The electricity is gone, but otherwise we're fine," she replied. "It was a tornado, wasn't it?"

"Yeah, it was. We could see it out the office window. I knew it didn't hit our neighborhood directly, but it wasn't far from it either. I was so scared! I'm going to try to get home right away, but it may take a while. There are probably a lot of fallen trees and other debris on the roads. I'll be there is soon as I can. I love you, honey—hug the kids for me. See you soon."

Almost an hour later, George arrived home. As he opened his front door, he realized that the lights had not yet come back on. Joan and the kids ran to him. After hugging everyone, he said, "You kids stay in here with the candles—I have to talk to Mommy for a minute." Taking Joan into the kitchen, George said "On the way home, I heard on the radio that there has been a terrible accident. A bus from the high school was going up Mount Jensen Road when the tornado hit it. It was blown over the guardrail and rolled almost 100 feet down the side of the hill. The driver and twenty-six kids on board were all killed!"

Materials Needed

Greeting cards with no message, stamps, pens, birthday candles, modeling clay

∂ ∂ ∂

George and Joan explain to the two older kids what has happened. They ask each other what they would do if a member of their family had been on the bus. Joan is especially unnerved and wants to do something. "What can we do?" she keeps asking herself. The next morning, she sees that the names of the victims have been printed in the local newspaper. The family has prayed for them, but she wants to do more. Susan asks if she can mail cards to some of the victim's families. This gives George an idea.

Going to the local drugstore, he purchases four dozen blank greeting cards. Gathering the family together, George spreads the cards out on the living room table. He mentions Susan's idea of writing to some of the families of the victims. He suggests that they write to all of them. Tim says he thinks this idea is okay, but can't think what to write. This brings the family to a discussion about what would be comforting to the families during this time. Susan suggests that just knowing that someone cares and took the time to write might make them feel better. They will realize that the community cares about them, and that they are not alone.

After their discussion, they each choose a card and a name from the newspaper. Before they begin writing, Tim suggests that everyone, including little Linda, place their hands on the stack of cards and that they have a moment of silence for the families. During the silence a prayer is said, asking for divine comfort for their terrible losses.

In a long cylinder of modeling clay, Joan has placed twenty-seven birthday candles that George had also bought at the drugstore. As they finish writing a note and addressing each card, family members light one of the candles for each of the deceased victims.

Variation

Because a tragedy of this seriousness takes so long to move beyond, Joan suggests that as a family they send cards once a month over the next three or four months. "You never know who will need the words that you write at that moment." They all agree to do this. When Joan speaks with her neighbor across the street about the accident, she explains what they have done as a family. The neighbor asks if her family might join them. Soon word gets around their intimate neighborhood, and six families join them the next month and a few more the month after. As a result, everyone feels more connected to the community as a whole.

chapter 15

Imaginative Family Problem Solving

In the preceding chapters, we have presented sixty-six activities we hope that you and your family will find useful. We are convinced, nevertheless, that the rituals you will enjoy most are the ones that you cooperate in designing yourselves. Children especially respond to being involved. The same kids who refuse to participate in a "family meeting" seem inspired when they are encouraged to figure out how to create a ritual. If your family is able to come up with a really imaginative ceremony, one that truly fits the needs of the situation, the gains you achieve from it and your dedication to using it are magnified. It is transformed into that most valuable of family possessions—a tradition.

In this last chapter, we depart from that format. Here we present three concepts, with illustrative activities, that will help your family to become more adept at imaginative problem solving. They are not in the form of rituals. Rather they are straightforward exercises meant to help your family become a creatively effective group of ritual designers.

Concept 1: "Out-of-the-Box" Thinking

When faced with an unspecific problem such as how to design an excellent ritual, most of us get stuck in a mental box, confined by a set of assumptions that we impose upon ourselves. Perhaps the ambiguity of the situation makes us overly cautious.

An ambiguous situation is one in which there are no guidelines to help you make decisions. Relevant facts are missing. The rules are unclear. You are uncertain as to as to how you should proceed. The first day of kindergarten is an example of an ambiguous situation for a five-year-old. For a sixteen-year-old, the first day on a new job fits that description.

People react differently to ambiguous situations. A circumstance that causes heightened interest in some individuals may cause great tension and anxiety in others. The ability to remain calm and open-minded in the face of ambiguity has been shown to promote imagination.

Family Activity

The Nine Dot Problem is an example of an ambiguous problem that you and your family might like to try (next page). To solve this problem, all nine dots must be connected with four straight lines, without letting your pen or pencil leave the paper. Solution is in the Appendix.

Creativity expert Paul Torrance describes why the Nine Dot Problem is an example of tolerance of ambiguity:

> Most people assume that the nine dots form a square and that the solution must be found within the square, *a self-imposed condition*. One's failure does not lie in the impossibility of the task, but in the attempted solutions. A person will continue to fail as long as he [feels forced to "stay inside the box"]. Solutions become easy once one breaks away

The Nine Dot Problem

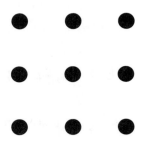

from the image of the square and looks outside of the nine dots. The solution involves leaving the "field" [the "box"].

What has all this to do with ritual invention? Situations that benefit from rituals frequently involve "thinking outside the box." In this section, we will explain two of the best methods for out-of-the-box thinking: *producing remote associates* and *lateral thinking.*

Producing Remote Associations

Perhaps the greatest problem families have when designing rituals is that they tend to accept the first idea that someone suggests. "Okay, sure," Mom will say, "let's give it a try." She is so happy that one of her kids is actively participating that she will go along with almost any idea. That's fine at the beginning, but the first idea that any of us produces is usually not of high quality. First ideas tend to be ordinary. Research on imaginative problem solving has shown that it usually takes a minimum of four to seven tries to generate an original thought.

Think about it. Isn't it true that when you and your partner try to solve a problem, you rarely think of more than two or three possible solutions? Then one or the other of you says, "All right, I can go along with that." You never get to see how good your thinking might be if you push yourselves for some unusual, possibly risky solutions. Even silly ideas, the research shows, often foster a good follow-up suggestion, perhaps in someone else's mind. You have to *play around* with the problem for a while to get a solution that will work in the long run.

It's the same with ritual design. When you and your family are attempting to dream up a great new rite, observe these two rules to encourage idea generation:

1. No *criticizing or making fun of someone else's ideas.*
2. No *self-editing your own ideas. If you think it, say it!*

A group was once trying to think of imaginative ways to get rid of old smashed auto glass, and someone said, "Melt it and spin it like cotton candy—it might be pretty." Some laughed, but it provided one fellow with a flash of insight. This is how fiberglass was invented!

Psychologists call the ideas you get after more than a few tries "remote associates." Such ideas are "remote" because they move away from traditional ways of thinking, and they're "associates" because they are linked in strange and unpredictable ways to more ordinary notions.

Family Activity

Here is an exercise that you and those in your family who are old enough (age nine or so) might try. The answers are in the Appendix. Once you see how it works, you can also invent easier versions for younger children.

The Remote Associates Test

Instructions: In this test you are presented with three words and asked to find a fourth word that is related to the other three. Write this word in the space to the right. For example, what word do you think is related to these three?

| cookies | sixteen | heart | _____ |

The answer in this case is *sweet*. Cookies are sweet; *sweet* is part of the phrase "sweet sixteen" and part of the word "sweetheart."

Here is another example:

| poke | go | molasses | _____ |

You should have written *slow* in the space provided. "Slow poke," "go slow," "slow as molasses." As you can see, the fourth word may be related to the other three for various reasons. Now try these. (Solution is in the Appendix)

1.	flap	tire	beanstalk	_____
2.	mountain	up	school	_____
3.	package	cardboard	fist	_____
4.	surprise	line	party	_____
5.	madman	acorn	bolt	_____
6.	telephone	high	electric	_____
7.	hair	income	fish	_____
8.	cream	bulb	heavy	_____

9. up	knife	Band-Aid	_____
10. snow	wash	black	_____
11. out	home	jail	_____
12. slugger	belfry	ball	_____
13. stage	game	actor	_____
14. Roman	arithmetic	one	_____
15. cat	color	holes	_____
16. belle	snow	beach	_____

This brief test gives you a taste of what remote associates feel like. If you were to invent your own test like this one, you would get more practice. Then you could transfer this ability to your design of rituals. For example, someone makes a suggestion that you light candles for a ceremony dedicated to discovering the family's heritage. For most people, that would be fine. But if you know that seeking remote associations gets to better ideas, you wouldn't be satisfied with this suggestion. You would ask the group for more contributions. Perhaps someone eventually volunteers that kerosene lanterns are more likely to evoke a sense of the past and thus would be more appropriate for such a ceremony. Remember, remote associates are not just more ideas, they're ideas that you have to force yourself to dig down into your mind for. John's research demonstrates that simply practicing this concept helps you think more creatively. This is also true of another "out-of the-box" concept, lateral thinking.

Lateral Thinking

Lateral thinking is similar to producing remote associates. Imagine that any problem solving, including ritual design, is like digging a hole. When we try to come up with a plan, we start digging away to find something that will work. We often use solutions that we have tried in the past when faced with the same kinds of problem. In other words, we stay right where we are, wrestling with the same basic idea, stuck in the same hole. Lateral thinkers, on the other hand, make mental jumps to the side of the original hole (hence the term "lateral") and begin digging a new one. They attempt to see the problem from a new angle. They endeavor to get a fresh start. Once they have brainstormed a number of innovative possibilities, they reorganize their ideas in order to determine the best solution. We will now suggest a couple of games that should help your family get a handle on lateral thinking, but any path that gets you there is a good one!

Family Activity

This activity is most effective for families with young or non-reading children. To do it, you will need a doll or stuffed animal, some toys, and some modeling clay or Play-Doh. Gather around the kitchen table (or in a play area) with your family. Take a stuffed animal or doll that is important to your child and place it next to him or her at the table. Across from the animal, use the toys that you brought to set up a "problem." For example, if you have a stuffed bear you could place a small jar of honey at the other end of the table and build a short wall in front of it with blocks or Lincoln Logs. Explain to your child that the bear would really like to go get the honey from across the table, but that he can't because there is a wall in front of it. Then show the clay to your child and ask him or her to create some objects out of it that could help the bear get the honey.

Your child might come up with a number of objects that could help the bear get the honey, such as a ladder, a trampoline, or a long rope to use as a lasso. Another way of approaching this activity is for you to create the objects yourself and then ask your child how he or she could use the object to help the bear.

Once your child has created several objects, you might want to change some of the elements in the story. For example, you could take the wall away and tell your child that there is now an angry swarm of bees circling the honey. Your child must now imagine a new way for the bear to get the honey, this time considering the threat of the bees rather than the wall. He or she could design a large net to capture the bees, or make a larger jar of honey that will distract the bees from the smaller jar that the bear wants.

This activity should help your child to think more flexibly about the problem, since he or she will have to change some of the prior ways of approaching the dilemma. Remember, it is fine if these solutions are very imaginative, or even a little unrealistic. The important thing is to help your family be as creative as possible and to solve problems in unconventional ways.

Family Activity

This activity is most effective in families with older, reading-age children. To do it, you will need a magic marker and a deck of index cards. Prior to beginning the activity, you will write one random word on each of the cards, making sure that you have an equal number of nouns and verbs. Feel free to be as creative as possible with your word selections. Place these cards in two piles according to parts of speech.

When your family gets together, each person draws one card from each of the piles.

Then one of the children makes up a sentence that contains the two words he or she has drawn. This sentence will be the first line of a story. Next an adult uses his or her cards to create a second sentence, which is constructed as logically as possible to follow the idea expressed in the first sentence of the story. As people take turns, drawing new cards as required, they make up a new sentence to continue the story.

In anticipation of their turn, they may develop a sentence in their minds already. However, when they hear the sentence before theirs, they will be forced quickly to rethink the direction of the story in order to incorporate the two new words they have drawn. In this way, family members soon learn to switch from linear, logical thinking into more creative, lateral thinking. Thus this activity provides practice for your family in rapidly shifting mental gears.

What has this got to do with designing family rites? Well, it gives participants practice in mental gymnastics. That is, it helps them to have confidence in making imaginative changes in direction as the group proceeds with the design. It also assures children that you want them to dare to deviate from expressing only predictable ideas and to let their imaginations soar. You won't always get reasonable suggestions this way, but it's easier to tone down an illogical notion than to try to improve mediocre ones.

Concept 2: A Parenting Style That Fosters Imagination

In addition to trying to help your family think outside the box, you can also foster imagination by the ways in which you interact with your children. One approach that you might want to consider is called the "nurturing parent" style of raising kids.

John has conducted an extensive study of families whose children were nominated by their school systems as being extremely imaginative. One hundred children in fifty-six New England families took part. Participating families were compared to twenty other families in which no one was identified as being especially creative.

The children in the main study and their parents each participated separately in two hours of interviews on the family's lifestyle. When we analyzed this massive amount of data, we had many insights into how a family's imagination may be fostered. In the course of the study, we learned that the families of the highly imaginative children were skilled communicators who enjoyed getting together for meetings to discuss a variety of issues. They had learned to trust one another thoroughly. They often spoke of rituals that they had invented because they believed doing so made their families special. Other findings included:

- *Rules for behavior.* The parents of the imaginative children averaged less than one specific rule for their children's behavior, such as number of study hours, bedtimes, or hours of TV watched. The group of twenty families with no highly imaginative members averaged six rules. The parents of the creative youth were not permissive, however. Permissive parents are those who exert little control over their children's behavior and fail to discipline them. The parents we studied were not the opposite type, either—authoritarian parents who exert strict control over their children.

We identified the families in this study as "nurturing parents."

These parents espoused and modeled a clear set of values and encouraged their children to decide for themselves what they should do to exemplify those values. As one father put it, "I can't think of any rules we've had for our kids—we just wanted each to become a 'Mensch' (a person the community admires)." Most of these parents remarked that they had surprisingly few problems with discipline.

- *Humor.* Joking, trick-playing, and family "fooling around" took an important place in these families. Family members often had comical names for each other and used a vocabulary understood only by them.

- *Housing.* Most of the families lived in decidedly different kinds of houses from other people. Many were modernistic; some were deck houses on rocky ledges in the woods, for example. Others were quite old; one family lives in a converted nineteenth-century town hall. Another bought a two-room eighteenth-century home, then added ultra-modern bedrooms and kitchen to the back of it. The furnishings of their homes were usually quite different, too. Several were decorated with surprising collections, such as Turkish teapots. In one home, a room was devoted to housing forty-seven unusual birds.

- *Practice making judgments* Probably one of the most important things that these families had in common was their rejection of the belief that "children are to be seen and not heard." To the contrary, they felt strongly that children should have an important role in the family's decision making. By allowing their children a lot of latitude, the parents gave them many opportunities to practice making judgments. This factor clearly contributed heavily to the children's success in the world. Of course, practice making judgments is exactly what happens when families engage regularly in designing their own rituals.

So what are the implications of this study for ritual design? It seems to us there are several:

- Have as few rules governing the design process as you can.

- Encourage a humorous approach, not only in the way you design, but also in the way that you carry out your ceremonies.

- Decorate your house as imaginatively as possible— that fosters the imagination of its occupants.

- Look for opportunities to reinforce your family for saying what they honestly think. Reward free and open expression of ideas.

Concept 3: Isaksen's Guidelines for Imaginative Thinking

As a final piece of advice on cultivating imaginitive problem solving, we have adapted a set of guidelines published by Scott Isaksen in the *Journal of Creative Behavior.* These actions reflect the concepts of out-of-the-box thinking and nurturing parenting.

- Help family members reduce pressure on each other and provide a nonpunitive environment.

- Tolerate disorder of it does not jeopardize health and safety.

- Encourage everyone to support and reinforce unusual ideas; praise the value of each person's contributions to your ritual plans.

- Help family members to realize that imaginative thinking is always a work in progress; there is no right or wrong way.

- Allow time for them to think about and develop their imaginative ideas. Problem solving seldom occurs spontaneously.

- Create a climate of mutual respect and acceptance so that your family will share, develop, and learn from one another.

- Encourage imaginative activities by being a resource rather than a controller.

- A warm and humorous atmosphere provides freedom and security in exploratory thinking.

- Encourage and use provocative questions; move away from the use of "right answer" questions.

- Remember, we like are the turtle in that we never get anywhere unless we stick our necks out!

In Summary

We can think of no better way to summarize the philosophy of our book than this poem by environmental poet Wendell Berry:

> *Within the circles of our lives*
> *we dance the circles of the years,*
> *the circles of the seasons*
> *within the circles of the years,*
> *the cycles of the moon*

within the circles of the seasons,
the circles of our reasons
within the cycles of the moon.

Again, again we come and go
changed, changing.
Hands join, unjoin in love and fear,
grief and joy. The circles turn,
each giving into each, into all.
Only music keeps us here,
each by all the others held.
In the hold of hands and eyes
we turn in pairs, that joining
joining each to all again.
And then we turn aside, alone,
out of the sunlight gone
into the darker circles of return.

We wish you and your family great success in crafting rituals that enrich your lives and make them more joyful!

Appendix: Solutions to Problems

Solution The Nine Dot Problem

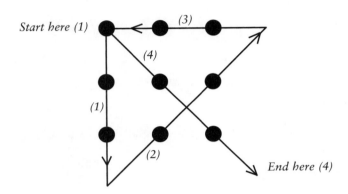

Solutions to the Remote Associates Test

1. jack
2. grade, high
3. box
4. party
5. nut
6. wire
7. net
8. light
9. cut
10. white
11. home
12. bat
13. play
14. numeral
15. black
16. ball

Recommended Resources

General Sources

Bell, C. *Ritual: Perspectives and Dimensions.* New York: Oxford University Press, 1997.

Berry, W. "Circle of Our Lives." In *Earth Prayers,* E. Roberts (ed.). San Francisco: Harper, 1991.

Biziou, B. *The Joy of Ritual: Spiritual Recipes to Celebrate Milestones, Ease Transitions, and Make Every Day Sacred.* New York: Golden Books Publishing Company, 1999.

Doty, W. *Mythography.* Montgomery, AL: University of Alabama Press, 1986.

Driver, T. *The Magic of Ritual: Our Need for Liberating Rites That Transform Our Lives and Our Communities.* New York: HarperCollins, 1993.

Fulghum, R. *From Beginning to End: The Rituals of Our Lives.* New York: Villard Books, 1995.

Grimes, R. *Marrying & Burying: Rites of Passage in a Man's Life.* Boulder, CO: Westview Press, 1995.

Lieberman, S. *New Traditions: Redefining Celebrations for Today's Family.* New York: Farrar, Straus & Giroux (Noonday Press), 1991.

Linn, D. *Sacred Space: Clearing and Enhancing the Energy of Your Home.* New York: Ballantine Books, 1996.

Luhrs, J. *The Simple Living Guide: A Sourcebook for Less Stressful, More Joyful Living.* New York: Broadway Books, 1997.

Rappaport, R. *Ritual and Religion in the Making of Humanity.* Cambridge, U.K. & New York: Cambridge University Press, 1999.

St. James, E. *Inner Simplicity: 100 Ways to Regain Peace and Nourish Your Soul.* New York: Hyperion, 1995.

St. James, E. *Simplify Your Life: 100 Ways to Slow Down and Enjoy the Things That Really Matter.* New York: Hyperion, 1994.

Segal, R. *The Myth and Ritual Theory: An Anthology.* Malden, MA: Blackwell Publishers, 1998.

Taylor, R., S. Seton, and D. Greer. *Simple Pleasures.* Berkeley, CA: Conari Press, 1996.

Torevell, D. *Losing the Sacred: Ritual, Modernity and Liturgical Reform.* Edinburgh: T & T Clark, 2000.

Altars

Bennett, D. *The Altar Call: Its Origins and Present Usage.* Lanham, MD: University Press of America, 2000.

Denburg, J. *Altar of the Seasons.* Buffalo, NY: Mosaic Press, 1995.

McMann, J. *Sacred Spaces: Altars and Icons.* San Francisco: Chronicle Books, 1998.

Streep, P. *Altars Made Easy: A Complete Guide to Creating Your Own Sacred Space.* San Francisco: Harper, 1997.

About personal altars Web site: *www.divineimages.com/altars.html*

Ancient altars Web site: *dosaweb.faunce.wmich.edu/ORG/ancient altars*

The heart and meaning of women's altars Web site: *www.webstoreusa.com/atbooks/052/0521554705shtml*

Home altars Web site: *www.homealtars.com*

Men's Rituals

Badinter, E.; Davis, L. (trans). *On Masculine Identity.* New York: Columbia University Press, 1995.

Glennon, W. *Fathering.* Berkeley, CA: Conari Press, 1995.

Rites of Passage

Blumenkrantz, D., and S. Gavazzi. "Guiding Transitional Events for Children and Adolescents through a Modern Day Rite of Passage," *Journal of Primary Prevention* 13:3 (1993), 199–212.

Close, H. "From Home to Nursing Home: A Ritual of Transition," *American Journal of Family Therapy* 23:1 (1995), 83–88.

Coles, R. *The Spiritual Life of Children*. Boston: Houghton Mifflin, 1991.

Gavazzi, S., and D. Blumenkrantz. "Facilitating Clinical Work with Adolescents and Their Families through the Rite of Passage Experience Program," *Journal of Family Psychotherapy* 4:2 (1993), 47–67.

Goblet-Vanormelingen, V. *La maison du mbombo: rite thérapeutique pour les enfants a hauts risques dans le Zaire rural.* ("The House of Mbombo: A Therapeutic Ritual for High-Risk Children in Rural Zaire"), *Social Science and Medicine* 37:2 (1993), 241–52.

Hollis, J. *The Middle Passage: From Misery to Meaning in Midlife.* Toronto: Inner City Books, 1993.

Isaacs, T. "The Archetypal Nature of Christian Initiation," *Pastoral Psychology* 42:3 (1994), 163–70.

Meske, C., G. Sanders, W. Meredith and D. Abbott. "Perceptions of Rituals and Traditions among Elderly Persons," *Activities, Adaptation and Aging* 18:2 (1994), 13–26.

Peteet, J. "Male Gender and Rituals of Resistance in the Palestinian Intifada: A Cultural Politics of Violence," *American Ethnologist* 21:1 (1994), 31–49.

Wall, K, and G. Ferguson. *Lights of Passage: Rituals and Rites of Passage for the Problems and Pleasures of Modern Life.* San Francisco: HarperCollins, 1994.

White, M. "Ritual of Inclusion: An Approach to Extreme Uncontrolled Behavior in Children and Young Adolescents," *Journal of Child and Youth Care* 9:2 (1994), 51–64.

Ritual Elements

Grey Wolf. *Earth Signs: How to Connect with the Natural Spirits of the Earth*. New York: Daybreak Books, 1998.

McArthur, M. *Wisdom of the Elements*. Freedom, CA: Crossing Press, 1998.

Oman, M. (Ed.). *Prayers for Healing*. Berkeley, CA: Conari Press, 1997.

Rituals for Families

Benson, P., J. Galbraith, and P. Espeland. *What Kids Need to Succeed: Proven, Practical Ways to Raise Good Kids*. Minneapolis, MN: Free Spirit Publishing, 1998.

Biziou, B. *The Joy of Family Ritual: Recipes for Everyday Living*. New York: St. Martin's Press, 2000.

Cox, C., and C. Evatt. *Simply Organized! How to Simplify Your Complicated Life*. New York: Perigee Press, 1998.

Cox, M. *The Heart of a Family*. New York: Random House, 1998.

Chesto, K. *Family Prayer for Family Times: Traditions, Celebrations, and Ritual*. Mystic, CT: Twenty Third Publications, 1995.

Doe, M., and M. Walch, *The Ten Principles of Spiritual Parenting*. New York: Harperperennial Library, 1998.

Eyre, L. and R. *Three Steps to a Strong Family*. New York: Simon & Schuster, 1994.

Frank, A. *Bless This House: A Collection of Blessings to Make a House Your Home*. Chicago: Contemporary Books, 1996.

Gillias, J. *A World of Their Own Making: Myth, Ritual, and the Quest for Family Values*. San Francisco: HarperCollins, 1996.

Godfrey, N. *A Penny Saved: Teaching Your Children the Values and Life Skills They Will Need to Live in the Real World*. New York: Fireside, 1996.

Klein, T. *Celebrating Life*. Oak Park, IL: Delphi, 1992.

Lew, A. and B. L. Bettner, *Raising Kids Who Can*. Newton Center, MA: Connexions Press, 1990.

Lockwood, G. *The Complete Idiot's Guide to Organizing Your Life*. New York: Alpha Books, 1996.

McCullough, B. *401 Ways to Get Your Kids to Work at Home*. New York: St. Martin's Press, 1982.

Morgenstern, J. *Organizing from the Inside Out*. New York, NY: Owl Books, 1998.

Nichols, T., and C. Jacques. "Family Reunions: Communities Celebrate New Possibilities." In Friedman, S. (ed), *The Reflecting Team in Action: Collaborative Practice in Family Therapy. Guilford Family Therapy Series*. New York: Guilford Press, 1995, pp. 314–30.

Ochs, E., and C. Taylor, "Family Narrative as Political Activity," *Discourse and Society* no. 3 (1992), 301–40.

Pipher, M. *The Shelter of Each Other*. New York: Ballantine Books, 1996.

Roberto, J. *Family Rituals and Celebrations: A Guide*. New Rochelle, NY: Don Bosco Multimedia, 1992.

St. James, E. *Simplify Your Life with Kids*. Kansas City, MO: Andrews McMeel Publishing, 2000.

Vogt, S. *Just Family Nights: 60 Activities to Keep Your Family Together in a World Falling Apart*. Elgin, IL: Brethren Press, 1994.

Women's Rituals

Adelman, P. *Miriam's Well: Rituals for Jewish Women around the Year*. Fresh Meadows, NY: Biblio Press, 1986.

Eiker, D. and Sapphire. *Keep Simple Ceremonies*. Portland, ME: The Feminist Spiritual Community, 1995.

Libra, K. *Creating Circles of Power and Magic: A Woman's Guide to Sacred Community*. Freedom, CA: Crossing Press, 1994.

Louden, J. *The Woman's Comfort Book: A Self-Nurturing Guide for Restoring Balance in Your Life*. San Francisco: Harper, 1992.

Stein, D. *Casting the Circle*. Freedom, CA: Crossing Press, 1990.
_____. *The Goddess Celebrates*. Freedom, CA: Crossing Press, 1991.

Telesco, P. *The Wiccan Book of Ceremonies and Rituals*. Secaucus, NJ: Carol Publishing Group, 1999.

Van Steenhouse, A. *A Woman's Guide to a Simpler Life*. New York: Random House, 1997.

Walker, B. *Women's Rituals*. San Francisco: Harper & Row, 1990.

Acknowledgments

When a book is largely made up of newly invented concepts, as this one is, it should not be surprising that many people had a hand in producing it. The authors would like to acknowledge and express their deep gratitude to the following: Jennifer Allen, Kristen Dacey-Iwai, Linda Dacey, Tara Dry, Juliette Fay, Marsia Hill, Wendy Hubenthal, Christine Kelly, Alison McConologue, Rebecca Michaels, Dr. Janet Morganelli, Carrie Payne, Stacy Phelan, Shelley Quilty, Brian Rotstein, Bridget Shanley, Lauren Szewczyk, Mark Tinkham, and Patrick Weygint.

We especially wish to thank three individuals without whose help our book would be much the poorer: Terry DelPercio, Erica Lolli, and Robin Tartaglia.

At Conari Press, we are grateful for the efforts of Heather McArthur, Pam Suwinsky, Jenny Collins, Claudia Smelser, Brenda Knight, Don McIlraith, Leah Russell, Rosie Levy, and Julie Kessler.

Finally and foremost, we want to say how much we are indebted to the creativity and professional judgment of Conari's executive editor, Leslie Berriman.

Index

About the Authors

JOHN S. DACEY, Ph.D., is the father of three daughters and has five grandchildren. He is a professor at Boston College in the Department of Counseling and Developmental Psychology. A researcher in adolescent and adult development, he is the author of twelve books and nearly thirty articles on parenting, creativity, and general human development. His most recently published book is entitled *Your Anxious Child*. He is currently working on a book on rituals for helping individuals progress through 12-step programs.

Jenny Keegan

LYNNE WEYGINT is the mother of two sons, a professional organizer, and a religious educator. Through her work helping families develop organizational systems in their homes, she has found that the implementation of routines and rituals helps her clients as much as organizing the physical clutter. With coauthor John Dacey, Ms. Weygint has also helped other religious educators and individuals within her Unitarian Universalist community create their own rituals.

To Our Readers

CONARI PRESS publishes books on topics ranging from spirituality, personal growth, and relationships to women's issues, parenting, and social issues. Our mission is to publish quality books that will make a difference in people's lives—how we feel about ourselves and how we relate to one another. We value integrity, compassion, and receptivity, both in the books we publish and in the way we do business.

As a member of the community, we donate our damaged books to nonprofit organizations, dedicate a portion of our proceeds from certain books to charitable causes, and continually look for new ways to use natural resources as wisely as possible.

Our readers are our most important resource, and we value your input, suggestions, and ideas about what you would like to see published. Please feel free to contact us, to request our latest book catalog, or to be added to our mailing list.

2550 Ninth Street, Suite 101
Berkeley, California 94710-2551
800-685-9595   510-649-7175
fax: 510-649-7190   e-mail: conari@conari.com
http://www.conari.com